Hubert Lacey is a Professor of Psychiatry at the University of London and Clinical Director and Consultant of the St George's Eating Disorders Service in London, the Yorkshire Centre for Eating Disorders in Leeds, the Peninsula Eating Disorders Service in Exeter and at Capio Nightingale Hospital, also in London. He is a graduate of the universities of St Andrews, Dundee and London, and is a Fellow of the Royal College of Psychiatrists. He is Chairman of the European Council on Eating Disorders and is Patron of **beat** (previously the Eating Disorders Association), which is the user and carer charity for the UK. Professor Lacey has published over 140 publications on anorexia nervosa, bulimia nervosa, obesity and psychosomatic illness.

Christine Craggs-Hinton, mother of three, followed a career in the Civil Service until, in 1991, she developed fibromyalgia, a chronic pain condition. Christine took up writing for therapeutic reasons and has, in the past few years, produced *Living with Fibromyalgia, The Fibromyalgia Healing Diet, The Chronic Fatigue Healing Diet, Coping with Polycystic Ovary Syndrome, Coping with Gout, How to Beat Pain, Coping with Eating Disorders and Body Image, Living with Multiple Sclerosis, Coping with Tinnitus, Coping with Hearing Loss* and *Coping Successfully with Varicose Veins* (all published by Sheldon Press). She also writes for the Fibromyalgia Association UK and the related *FaMily* magazine. In recent years she has become interested in fiction writing, too.

Kate Robinson is a research assistant attached to the St George's Eating Disorders Service. A psychologist by training, Kate spent two years nursing severely ill anorectics. Her research tests the efficacy of different treatment approaches.

Overcoming Common Problems Series

Selected titles

A full list of titles is available from Sheldon Press,
36 Causton Street, London SW1P 4ST and on our website at
www.sheldonpress.co.uk

Body Language: What You Need to Know
David Cohen

The Complete Carer's Guide
Bridget McCall

The Confidence Book
Gordon Lamont

Coping Successfully with Period Problems
Mary-Claire Mason

Coping with Age-related Memory Loss
Dr Tom Smith

Coping with Chemotherapy
Dr Terry Priestman

Coping with Compulsive Eating
Ruth Searle

Coping with Diverticulitis
Peter Cartwright

Coping with Family Stress
Dr Peter Cheevers

Coping with Hearing Loss
Christine Craggs-Hinton

Coping with Heartburn and Reflux
Dr Tom Smith

Coping with Macular Degeneration
Dr Patricia Gilbert

Coping with Radiotherapy
Dr Terry Priestman

Coping with Tinnitus
Christine Craggs-Hinton

The Depression Diet Book
Theresa Cheung

Depression: Healing Emotional Distress
Linda Hurcombe

Depressive Illness
Dr Tim Cantopher

The Fertility Handbook
Dr Philippa Kaye

Helping Children Cope with Anxiety
Jill Eckersley

How to Approach Death
Julia Tugendhat

How to Be a Healthy Weight
Philippa Pigache

How to Get the Best from Your Doctor
Dr Tom Smith

How to Make Life Happen
Gladeana McMahon

How to Talk to Your Child
Penny Oates

The IBS Healing Plan
Theresa Cheung

Living with Autism
Fiona Marshall

Living with Eczema
Jill Eckersley

Living with Heart Failure
Susan Elliot-Wright

Living with Loss and Grief
Julia Tugendhat

Living with a Seriously Ill Child
Dr Jan Aldridge

The Multiple Sclerosis Diet Book
Tessa Buckley

Overcoming Emotional Abuse
Susan Elliot-Wright

Overcoming Hurt
Dr Windy Dryden

The PMS Handbook
Theresa Cheung

Simplify Your Life
Naomi Saunders

Stress-related Illness
Dr Tim Cantopher

The Thinking Person's Guide to Happiness
Ruth Searle

The Traveller's Good Health Guide
Dr Ted Lankester

Treat Your Own Knees
Jim Johnson

Treating Arthritis – The Drug-Free Way
Margaret Hills

Overcoming Common Problems

Overcoming Anorexia

PROFESSOR J. HUBERT LACEY,
CHRISTINE CRAGGS-HINTON
and
KATE ROBINSON

sheldon **PRESS**

First published in Great Britain in 2007

Sheldon Press
36 Causton Street
London SW1P 4ST

The author and publisher have made every effort to ensure that the
external website and email addresses included in this book are correct and
up to date at the time of going to press. The author and publisher are not
responsible for the content, quality or continuing accessibility of the sites.

British Library Cataloguing-in-Publication Data
A catalogue record for this book is available from the British Library

ISBN 978-0-85969-986-0

1 3 5 7 9 10 8 6 4 2

Typeset by Fakenham Photosetting Ltd, Fakenham, Norfolk
Printed in Great Britain by Ashford Colour Press

Produced on paper from sustainable forests

Contents

Note to the reader   vi

1 Anorexia defined   1

2 The psychological dimension   11

3 The behavioural dimension   17

4 The physiological dimension   27

5 The causes of anorexia   35

6 Signs to watch out for   45

7 Fertility and pregnancy   49

8 Treatment   61

9 Helping yourself   82

Appendix: Weight charts   115

Useful addresses   117

Note to the reader

This is not a medical book and is not intended to replace advice from your doctor. Consult your doctor if you believe you have any of the symptoms described, and if you think you might need medical help.

1

Anorexia defined

Anorexia nervosa is one of the eating disorders, yet people with anorexia do not have a problem with their eating! They can chew or eat their food as well as anyone. They do, however, have a problem with their thinking and their emotions. The name 'anorexia nervosa' literally means 'nervous loss of appetite', but this is misleading. People with anorexia (the term used by the medical profession is 'anorectic') are almost always hungry. But they deny their hunger through sheer will-power and stubborn single-mindedness.

It is often easier to say what anorexia isn't rather than what it is. It is not a 'slimmers' disease', nor does it develop because people want to look attractive. People with anorexia have a powerful psychiatric disorder that alters the way they think; it makes them irrational and drives them into a dangerous medical state. It is a complicated disorder where the mind alters the body and vice versa. Someone once said that anorexia is not a problem but a solution to a problem.

Many eating disorders are described in medical books but there are four main ones. In addition to anorexia nervosa, there is bulimia nervosa, binge-eating disorder, and EDNOS or eating disorder not otherwise specified. Bulimia (literally 'the appetite of an ox') involves frequent binge-eating coupled with compensatory behaviours designed to avoid gaining weight. Binge-eating disorder involves frequent binge-eating without any compensatory behaviours. Hence, binge-eating disorder is usually associated with obesity, while bulimia nervosa occurs in people of a normal weight. EDNOS is a range of eating disorders including binge-eating disorder, and also includes eating disturbances that show some of the features of anorexia and bulimia but not all. Bulimia nervosa is sometimes confused with anorexia, but it is important to distinguish them because their treatment and prognosis are very different.

We hear a lot about anorexia nervosa but it is not a common disorder, although eating disorders as a whole are common indeed. About 0.7 per cent of girls and women aged between 15 and 30 years develop anorexia. Some men also develop anorexia, though the vast majority of people with anorexia are female.

Anorexia nervosa leads to many physical complications and it also has a high mortality rate. This has been variously estimated between 10 and 20 per cent. Indeed, anorexia is considered to have the highest rate of mortality among psychiatric conditions. It is surprising and concerning to note that the death rate of people with anorexia is higher than that of alcoholics or drug misusers.

Features of anorexia

Most people know something about the features of anorexia nervosa. Most, if asked, would say that people with anorexia are thin, and that they can't or won't eat. These are true, but the total picture is more complicated.

To make a diagnosis of anorexia, three main features need to be present. First, there needs to be a behaviour, such as dieting, which leads to weight loss. Second, the weight loss has to be sufficient that the person with anorexia, if female, stops menstruating, and has a low sexual drive. Lastly, the thinking of people with anorexia changes; they only feel comfortable at a low weight and become terrified of being at a normal weight.

Anorexia is diagnostically different from bulimia nervosa. Anorexia invariably begins in adolescence while bulimia is usually a condition of adulthood. People with bulimia are at normal weight, whereas people with anorexia are emaciated. Anorexia has a specific psychopathology involving a fear of normal weight while bulimics, though wishing to be slim, rarely want to lose more than a stone (6.3 kg). People with anorexia are brought to medical attention early because it is clear that something is amiss; bulimics on the other hand often spend five or seven years struggling before coming for help. Bulimia is comparatively easy to treat while the prognosis of anorexia, without treatment, is poor.

There are five main means by which people with anorexia lower their weight. The most common is dietary restriction. Almost as common is over-activity or excessive exercise: a person with anorexia may spend many hours a day in the gym or exercising in their room. Laxative and diuretic misuse are not common but, when they occur, can lead to dangerous problems. Vomiting is however commonly used. It is often preceded by a binge and occurs in about 60 per cent of people with anorexia. Those who induce vomiting tend to have a slightly poorer prognosis but the difference is not enough to be a concern.

A weight loss of between 6 and 12 kg will lead to most women developing irregular menstruation. Below 47 kg, most women's periods stop and below 42 kg they lose libido. At this weight the female hormones stop their cyclical activity and the ovaries become depleted and infertile, reverting to those of a young girl. The emaciation leads to physical changes such as dry skin and weak muscles. Bulimic anorectics who vomit develop a swelling in their salivary glands and their teeth can become eroded. All people with anorexia at low weight become dizzy and sensitive to cold. They are likely to wake early in the morning and are very restless. Their bones become demineralized of calcium and liable to fracture.

People with anorexia view weight in a quite different way from people of normal weight. They develop a special way of thinking that marks them out, not only from well people but also from all other people with psychiatric disorders: an irrational fear of normal body weight. It is not that they just dislike being overweight or wish to avoid being fat – for these are common in most people. Rather, it is an intense pursuit of thinness, a hatred of a normal weight and shape with a profound disparagement of the body.

People with anorexia retreat into their own world, becoming perfectionists and working long hours. They lose concentration; their thoughts are limited to food and weight; they give up their friends and distance themselves from their families. The boundaries of their world become very narrow.

All individuals with anorexia should try and help themselves. Getting better will be a struggle. It is frightening to gain weight, but there always comes a point when the problems of giving up anorexia are less than the problems of anorexia itself. People with anorexia should seek help speedily.

While this book is meant to inform and assist, someone with anorexia should always consult their doctor and, for most, specialist care is required.

Similar conditions with some symptoms in common

Phobic avoidance of normal body weight is the core psychological disturbance in anorexia. This is absent in bulimia nervosa, the condition with which it is most often confused, but there are other conditions which might be misinterpreted for anorexia:

- Being a picky eater. Children in particular have fads and refuse to eat certain foods. Weight loss, dieting behaviour, poor body image and so on are not present in this instance, so anorexia can be ruled out.
- Loss of weight and poor appetite. Someone who has these

symptoms yet doesn't have the other symptoms of anorexia may have an underlying medical disorder that needs urgent attention. A doctor must be consulted.

- Food Avoidance Emotional Disorder. This condition is believed to occur in some children prior to the possible onset of anorexia. There is less weight loss and the anorectic psychopathology is less pronounced. If the child receives help at this juncture, there is less likelihood of her going on to develop anorexia.
- Affective disorder. A person who is depressed – even a child – will lack appetite. She or he should see a doctor and be assessed for this condition.
- Selective eating. Some children in particular will exist on only two or three types of food, such as chocolate, crisps, biscuits or a specific type of sandwich. There is no weight loss or anorectic psychopathology.
- Pervasive Refusal Syndrome. This fairly rare condition is expressed by an abject refusal in many areas, including eating, drinking, walking, speaking and caring for oneself. Some of the symptoms of anorexia are shared, but the core disturbance is very different.

Who gets anorexia?

As we have seen, it is estimated that 0.7 per cent of women aged 15 to 30 years develop anorexia nervosa. Additionally, 1.8 per cent of women aged 15 to 40 develop bulimia nervosa. In total, 5 per cent of young women develop various forms of eating disorder, many of which self-limit; in other words there are brief periods of vomiting or laxative abuse that come to an end sometimes with, sometimes without, treatment. Furthermore, it is thought that 10 to 20 per cent of adolescent and young adult women exhibit some of the clinical symptoms, but not enough to be given a diagnosis.

It is estimated that each year there are 19 new cases of anorexia per 100,000 females and 2 new cases per 100,000 males. Figures provided by clinics suggest that 5 per cent of anorexia sufferers are male. There has been an assumption that anorexia is more common in gay communities, but in fact very few men with anorexia are homosexual.

More often than not, anorexia begins in adolescence or early adulthood, and the average age of onset is 15–16 years – a figure which appears to be slowly dropping. Although most people with anorexia are between the ages of 15 and 20 years, the condition has been seen in children as young as six as well as elderly adults.

Until recently, it was thought that anorexia was extremely rare in developing countries and uncommon in black populations. However, increasing evidence is showing that anorexia exists in many cultures, though the numbers are not yet clear. It is also unclear whether this is because anorexia is uncommon in these populations or whether it has simply not been detected.

The same is the case with respect to social classes. Until recently it was thought that anorexia is mainly found in middle-class groups. This may, however, indicate a degree of under-diagnosis of anorexia in the lower social classes, or perhaps that people with anorexia in this group are less able to seek or receive treatment and so present to clinics less frequently. In reality, anorexia is found in all social and ethnic groups.

People who work in circles where appearance is important and thinness is highly valued also have a greater chance of developing anorexia than those in other walks of life. These circles include industries such as fashion, music, television and film; ballet and modern dance; and sports such as athletics and gymnastics.

Eating disorders tend to run in families. In fact, anorexia is 12 times more likely than normal to arise when the person's mother or sisters has it. Moreover, when a close relative has anorexia, the people around her are three times more likely to develop it. In such instances, the cause can be one of the following, or a combination of the two:

• environmental, for example where family members share the same environment in which the mother and sister perhaps miss meals, strictly count calories, are conscious of body image and disparaging of those who are overweight;
• genetic, in other words some family members can inherit a predisposition to developing anorexia. Researchers are currently trying to isolate the gene or genes that cause a person to be at risk of anorexia.

The theory that there is a genetic element to anorexia has gained strength as a result of recent studies. In studies of identical twins with anorexia, both twins had the disorder in about 50 per cent of cases, but in studies of non-identical (fraternal) twins with anorexia, only 8 per cent both had the disorder. It's still not clear whether the passage of anorexia across the generations is due to nature or nurture.

No parental blame

If you are the parent of someone with anorexia, you may have heard that anorexia is caused by poor parenting and feel the fault is somehow yours. Please be aware that parenting issues are not generally a causative factor and that reports to this effect are a myth. There is no evidence at all to support them, as is clear from the many studies that have been carried out into identical twins, only one of whom has anorexia. The ratio of parents (of offspring with anorexia) with good to those with poor parenting skills is now believed to be similar to that in the general population.

What is the prognosis?

The outcome of anorexia, with or without treatment, depends on the individual and his or her motivation. Not even experts in the field can work out who will get better, or who will remain ill. Broadly speaking, prognosis is better when the individual is young and the history is short. The prognosis is not so good when there is a long history of the disorder and when severe weight loss has occurred. Some feel that severe binge-eating and vomiting indicates that treatment is likely to be more protracted.

Anorexia in males

There can be a misconception that eating disorders are a female phenomenon, which is made worse by the erroneous view, held in the past, that men with an eating disorder are likely to be gay. However, awareness that men can develop eating disorders is increasing, reducing the stigma associated with eating disorders and making it easier for men to ask for help.

Although men and women with an eating disorder behave in similar ways, in the past males were less likely to receive a correct diagnosis than females. They were more likely to have their concerns dismissed by their GP and more likely to be misdiagnosed by psychiatrists. Indeed, many were diagnosed as having depression with associated appetite changes, and so were not given the help they desperately needed. Diagnosis of males is slowly changing, however, as awareness is raised.

There has always been an emphasis on the way women look, but now men are being increasingly targeted by the media and the beauty industry to aspire to ideal body shapes. Unlike that of women, the ideal male body shape is muscular rather than thin (although there will always be individual variations). It is thought that athletic competition and activities that place emphasis on body shape and muscularity are likely to increase the risk of eating disorders in men.

Nevertheless, the course of anorexia is sufficiently similar in males and females that the majority of information in this book is relevant to both men and women who think they may have anorexia.

The history of anorexia

With rising incidence and diagnosis, the impression may be gained that anorexia is a fairly new disorder, a consequence of today's culture and increasing affluence. However, the condition is known to have been present for over a thousand years. Indeed, the writings of the European religious cult of St Wilgefortis between AD 700 and 1000 (see box) suggest that the clinical features, psychopathology and even treatment of anorexia were understood at that period.

In more recent times, Sir William Gull – one of the Victorian era's most eminent physicians – in 1874 gave the first modern, insightful descriptions of the condition, and it was he who termed it 'anorexia nervosa'. At the end of the nineteenth century there was a considerable interest in eating and weight disorders, but the diagnosis of anorexia nervosa was nevertheless rarely made. The condition became confused with tuberculosis and various hormone deficiencies.

It was not until after the Second World War that anorexia gradually came to be seen as a developmental issue, one often triggered by cultural messages about the 'ideal' body. By the 1980s the numbers of people diagnosed with anorexia had risen dramatically and public awareness had increased. In the anglophone world, three clinical researchers made major strides. These were Dr Hilde Bruch in the USA, and Professors Gerald Russell and Arthur Crisp in the UK. Their research on the aetiology and clinical management of anorexia has stood the test of time and the views of all three have influenced the contents of this book.

St Wilgefortis

According to legend, the seventh daughter of the pagan king of Portugal was a thoughtful Christian girl who was said to reject the 'worldly interests' of her sisters and devote her days to prayer. Her father was a tyrannical man who in some versions of the legend had an incestuous relationship with her. When she learnt of his plan to marry her to the king of Sicily, she was horrified. She had already made a solemn vow of chastity and planned to give her life to God, not man.

Desperate both to preserve her virginity and not to openly defy her father's command, she made impassioned prayers to God for help. She then became ascetic, meaning she followed the doctrine of extreme self-denial and austerity, which involved eating very little and becoming hyperactive. In addition, she begged the Lord to deprive her of all beauty, and he granted her prayer – by ridding her of her female shape and giving her a hairy body and a beard. (When a person becomes emaciated, downy hair called 'lanugo' grows on her body and her head hair will thin and fall out, emphasizing extraneous facial hair.)

As a result of Wilgefortis's unattractive appearance, the king of Sicily withdrew his suit, at which her father, in a rage, had her crucified. While on the cross she pleaded for women to remember the 'things suffered', which is thought to allude to menstruation and such. In later years, she was canonized and given the name Wilgefortis, which is Latin for 'strong virgin'.

When the cult of asceticism arrived in England, the statue of a female saint was erected in St Wilgefortis's honour in Billingsgate and called St Uncumber. (The legend of St Wilgefortis appears to have been told in various countries, and her name was different in each. This was perhaps because there were similar tales to tell in relation to other adolescent girls.) Sources from the Dark Ages referred to St Uncumber as a female saint who was prayed to exclusively by women to the derision of men.

There are earlier recorded cases of what we now call anorexia, but what is unique about the legend of St Wilgefortis is that the features of the disorder were clearly described. Moreover, it was an excellent attempt by unenlightened minds to explain how a series of well-born girls reacted to an overwhelming fear of the implications of sexuality and marriage.

2

The psychological dimension

Anorexia is a complex condition with three dimensions or layers – the psychological (affecting or arising in the mind), the behavioural (the way in which one conducts oneself), and the physiological (the way in which the body functions). Each of these dimensions is interwoven with the others, but it is helpful to separate them in order to try and understand the mind of the person with anorexia, and we will do so in this and the next two chapters. In this chapter we will be looking at the thought processes typical of people with anorexia.

The thinking or psychopathology of anorexia nervosa is dominated by a pursuit of thinness combined with disparagement and hatred of the body. The core element – one that doesn't occur in any other condition – is an irrational fear, or phobia, of normal body weight. People with anorexia have an intense fear of putting on weight, as opposed to a mere dislike. Furthermore, it is not obesity of which they are fearful, but normal body weight.

Typical thought processes

Rather than indulging in a range of hobbies and interests, people with anorexia shrink their boundaries – their thinking becomes limited to their diet and their need to lose weight. In addition, their sense of reality is distorted in that they define themselves solely by their ability to control their food intake. In addition to a fear of normal body weight, their psychological state is usually characterized by some or all of the following:

- Primarily, they think obsessively of food. They are fretful about what they have just eaten and anxious about what to eat next.
- They suffer intense and persistent anxiety over the way others see them. They constantly compare their bodies with those of others, and feel they're far fatter than others. They're also certain that others find them disgusting.
- They have 'black and white' thinking. In other words, they can only comprehend extremes of good and bad, right and wrong, and so on. Moreover, their capacity to discern shades of meaning disappears, and their ability to grasp rational arguments is greatly diminished. The only opinions and impressions they are able to consider are their own.
- Their minds are full of the same fixed and oversimplified thoughts, such as: 'If I get thin I'll be happy'; 'I don't deserve good things to happen to me because I'm overweight'; and 'If I eat normally, I'll have lost control'.
- Their thinking is immature in that they consider themselves resistant to the laws that govern all our lives. For instance, they accept that anorexia can lead to severe medical complications, but are convinced they are immune and that they uniquely will remain strong and healthy.
- Due to low self-esteem, they think very poorly of themselves. For instance, they believe they constantly draw attention from others who are disgusted by their overweight bodies.
- They are likely to suffer major mood swings, anxiety, depression and feelings of isolation.
- They develop a desire for perfection, which can translate to handwriting, homework and so on.
- They develop ritualistic behaviour, such as performing every single action in the same way every day, particularly actions relating to food, food preparation or exercise.

People with anorexia may express these psychological states in many different ways, but the following are some of the most common.

A strong drive to lose weight

Preoccupation with weight and a powerful need to be thin are overwhelming in anorexia, as the individual constantly and obsessively thinks up ways of shedding the kilograms (see below). For much of the time, where their weight is concerned, people with anorexia are either in heaven or hell. They are in heaven when they step on the scales and find they have lost a kilogram, and in hell when they find they have put on a little weight.

A preoccupation with food

As they plan each meal, people with anorexia are counting calories and arguing with themselves over whether they should cut out starchy foods even further. They are also thinking of the shopping they need and rehearsing in their minds exactly how they will prepare the meal. They will fill their free time by reading recipes for inspiration, watching TV cookery programmes and trawling through magazines for items related to food.

It's important to people with anorexia that they eat less than their mothers and sisters. After cooking a meal, they are liable to give others unreasonably large portions to ensure they themselves eat less. They make their meals last as long as possible by cutting the food into small pieces. The thought that they may at some point lose control and overeat haunts them constantly, and they are terrified of being pressurized into eating by family or friends. Their meals are therefore often eaten alone, away from the rest of the family.

When family celebrations come along which generally involve food, people with anorexia have to make excuses as to why their portions are smaller than everyone else's, why they don't want a slice of cake or an alcoholic drink – and so they dread such events. In time, they are likely to avoid each and every occasion where food might be involved, which contributes towards them feeling withdrawn and alone.

Rituals

As anorexia progresses, compulsive time-consuming rituals can arise. These often originate in the need to keep activity levels high, diverting attention from the physical discomfort of hunger. The rituals are each as unique as the person who conceives and implements them, and may include taking a shower after every meal, changing clothes every three hours or organizing food in the kitchen cupboards in an unnecessary, systematized way. Interestingly, ritual and obsessional thoughts are often reciprocal with symptoms of anorexia. Thus as the weight goes on, the rituals become more marked, and vice versa.

It's common for people with anorexia to develop strange eating habits, too, such as hiding food, refusing to eat in front of others, cutting food into tiny pieces, mashing it all up and eating in a particular pattern. They might rigorously watch the clock, performing all their tasks and activities at rigidly specific times, and always in the same way.

Some people with anorexia excuse themselves from their obsessional rules and impose them on others instead. This can make them extremely unforgiving towards others who are untidy, unpunctual and so on. Ultimately, they feel unable to cope with anyone who doesn't pander to their obsessions, and this makes them feel more isolated and alone. It also makes the people around them more frustrated and helpless.

Perfectionism

The desire to be perfect in every way is also a typical feature of anorexia. Female anorectics are the archetypal 'good girls', tending to be neat, tidy and very hardworking. They welcome order and handwriting can appear almost like calligraphy. In exams they are likely to achieve top grades as they work exceedingly hard. Sometimes parents may misunderstand this, seeing it as a beneficial trait instead of realizing that it's a part of an illness.

Social withdrawal

Individuals with anorexia find it difficult to be around other people. When in the company of others, they find it almost impossible to see their companions' point of view. If advice is given, they reject it immediately and feel very defensive. They assume that anyone who says they're thin is wrong. Moreover, they are often convinced that they don't have a distorted view of their appearance, but that the fault lies in other people. The fearful thought that friends may stop off for a pizza or curry makes them avoid going out with them. In time, it becomes very difficult for people with anorexia to be carefree and they may even refuse to see friends, cease taking phone calls and stop going out of the house. Some are so afraid of feeling the imagined fat on their bodies that they avoid touching their naked flesh. Others pinch their thighs or tummy repeatedly, frightened by what they feel and declaring they are fat. As the condition progresses, they can become increasingly isolated.

Stereotyped thinking

People with anorexia see the world in a different way from everyone else. Their sense of identity is dependent on the narrowest of factors, namely their ability to control their food intake and weight. Some repeat certain phrases over and over, like a chant. This prevents them from progressing from one thought or idea to another; it makes them unable to develop ideas, opinions and defences. This form of thinking comes across to their families as frustrating. They have a sense that the individual's thinking is endlessly going round in circles.

Depression

It is common for people with anorexia to feel sad, an emotion which becomes more pronounced as more weight drops off. Indeed, for some, low self-esteem and feelings of being worthless can propel the sadness into unmistakable depression. Persistent low mood, lack of energy, poor sleep, poor memory and concentration, and feelings of guilt are usually experienced, and the person can feel empty or dead inside.

Sometimes the word 'depression' is used as a euphemism for anger or marked anxiety. Anger is a very difficult emotion to put into words and it's hard to go to a doctor and say 'I'm angry!' All such feelings stem from the turmoil of anorexia.

Changed thinking at very low weight

At a variable point during weight loss, often around a body mass index (BMI) of 13 (see pages 27 and 32), the person's thinking processes become more disturbed, creating an altered state of consciousness. Indeed, it can appear to the family of a person with anorexia that her personality is changing. This altered state has the following characteristics:

- her thinking slows down;
- her speech becomes slow and slurred;
- her short-term memory becomes poor;
- her facial expression becomes vacant. She may appear 'punch-drunk' and lack the ability to focus;
- her judgement is poor and emotional responses abnormal, in the sense of being inappropriate or blunted.

When these changes in thinking occur, they represent a particular danger which the person with anorexia is unable to appreciate. For example she or he can't make rational decisions and can't understand his or her family's anxieties. In this scenario, immediate treatment in hospital is required which unfortunately may need to be compulsory.

3

The behavioural dimension

This chapter is concerned with the forms of behaviour most closely associated with anorexia, those aimed almost exclusively at achieving weight loss. These forms of behaviour can broadly be divided into the following categories:

- food restriction and, sometimes, binge-eating;
- behaviour focused on getting rid of food;
- behaviour focused on reducing the effects of ingested food;
- multi-impulsive behaviour, existing alongside anorexia.

We will now look in more detail at the specific forms these kinds of behaviours may take. Of course these categories are not mutually exclusive, and not every person with anorexia will display all these forms of behaviour.

Food restriction and binge-eating

Dietary restriction and its consequences

In anorexia, the main change in behaviour is food restriction. This is likely to begin with minor dieting episodes not dissimilar to those in which many young people engage – particularly girls. Then something 'clicks', and the individual becomes convinced that she would be much happier at a lower weight. She begins a very restrictive diet, one which she recognizes as being quite different from what has gone before and different from that which is common among young girls, for a firm resolve has lodged itself in her head. This is a rigid over-control of her food intake that gradually develops into anorexia.

In their drive to be thin, people with anorexia obsessively control the amount of food they eat. They may not yet be in their teens, but already they understand that fat contains more calories than other food groups. They therefore cut it out of their diet, professing that they are trying to eat healthily and that fat is bad for the heart. Most people with anorexia progressively eliminate different food groups from their diet. Carbohydrate foods, particularly bread, potatoes and pasta, are avoided and again their elimination is rationalized on health grounds. Some people with anorexia graduate to vegetarianism, or even become vegans as a further reason to avoid certain foods.

The things people with anorexia eat are usually small helpings of low-calorie foods such as vegetables, fruits, salads with non-oily dressings, cottage cheese and low-fat yoghurt. When anyone challenges them about the inadequacy of their diet, they are likely to say they know a lot about nutrition and are eating healthily by cutting out the bad things. They are unlikely to admit to being on a weight-loss programme. They are driven by a resolve to be at a lower weight with no rational view of when it will end. There is no target – seven, six, five stone is never enough.

People with anorexia will usually learn the calorific values of all the foods they eat, choosing only to eat the things with a small number of calories. As well as calorie counting, they may also set themselves perverse 'goals', saying to themselves something to the effect of, 'I will eat less than 1,000 calories a day, later reducing it to 800 and then 400'.

Use of 'diet pills'

Some people with anorexia use diet pills – drugs that suppress the appetite. Diet pills can produce unwanted side-effects such as chest pain, decreased ability to exercise, faintness, swelling of the feet or lower legs and difficulties with breathing. Serious heart or lung problems can arise when more diet pills than the brand recommends are taken over a prolonged period. Some appetite suppressants are habit-forming, particularly those that are derived from amphetamines, which are synthetic, mood-altering drugs. The habit leads to addiction, with all the psychological and physical consequences. Taking amphetamine-based diet pills also results in over-activity.

Binge-eating behaviour

Just as a dieter can lose resolve and hit a Mars bar, so too can the person with anorexia suddenly compensate for her starvation by binge-eating. The bulimic form of anorexia nervosa is the more common form – about 60 per cent of people with anorexia have it. Bulimic anorectics will at times give in to their ravenous hunger and abandon themselves to a binge-eating session, consuming a large amount of food in a short period of time. The foods eaten are typically high in fats and carbohydrates, but are consumed so quickly as not to be tasted and appreciated – they are often barely chewed. Immediately afterwards such individuals are wracked with fear. The only answer, as they see it, is to vomit back the food before the calories are absorbed. However, because their rigid control has been lost for a while, they feel guilty, utterly disgusted with themselves, a failure.

Binge-eating tends to be a secretive behaviour carried out in private and perceived as humiliating. Fridges are raided and food can even be stolen from supermarkets and the homes of family and friends.

Behaviour focused on getting rid of food

Self-induced vomiting

After a binge, people with anorexia are so distressed that they will generally make themselves vomit (purge). Usually the fingers are used and this gives rise to abrasions or calluses on the knuckles, known as Russell's sign. Even if Russell's sign is not present, the fingers are usually red and sometimes raw. This is a strong indication that the sufferer is vomiting. Vomiting can create a number of physical complications which are dealt with in Chapter 4.

Of course, purging behaviour leads to drastic weight loss. The individual will frequently step on and off the bathroom scales and often repeatedly measure and re-measure a particular part of the body, such as the wrists or ankles.

The behaviour of a person with anorexia can fluctuate dramatically. For example, such people may indulge in bulimic behaviour on and off for six months – despising themselves for it, as well as feeling terrified and guilty.

A combination of binge-eating and self-induced vomiting is the principal symptom of bulimia nervosa, but this is a quite different condition from anorexia nervosa. People with bulimia are at normal body weight, usually menstruate and lack the core psychopathology of anorexia, i.e. the fear of normal body weight as described in Chapter 2.

Misuse of laxatives

Misuse of laxatives is not uncommon in the general population. One study suggests that 10 per cent of women have used laxatives as an adjunct to dietary control. It is therefore unsurprising that laxative abuse is common among people with anorexia. Some find it difficult to make themselves sick so turn to laxatives instead, starting with a few tablets and increasing the dose to massive quantities as the bowel muscles become less able to function.

In time, laxative abuse upsets the normal mechanism of the digestive system, and the result can be constant diarrhoea, rectal bleeding and dehydration. It can also deplete sodium and potassium levels in the body (as do diuretics – see the next section), which can give rise to an irregular heartbeat. In some cases, heart failure can occur. Furthermore, laxative abuse interferes with the absorption of nutrients into the body, leading to severe nutritional deficiencies.

Conversely, if laxatives are stopped after months of misuse, normal bowel activity also stops, causing water retention, bloating and chronic constipation. People with anorexia who no longer misuse laxatives can find it takes many months or even years for the digestive system to function normally again. Some laxatives damage the many folds of the intestine, causing continuing problems such as pain, bleeding and poor absorption of nutrients.

What many people with anorexia don't realize is that laxatives are ineffective as a weight-loss technique, since most calories are absorbed in the upper digestive tract and most laxatives act on the lower digestive tract. For most people who abuse laxatives, they act as a diuretic. The weight reduction seen on the scales after taking laxatives is the result of fluid loss, the fluids being part of the resultant diarrhoea. However, this is a temporary effect as the person with anorexia inevitably gets thirsty and has a drink, which restores the fluid balance and returns the body weight to what it was previously.

Misuse of diuretics

Diuretics are pills designed to encourage urination and so to reduce water content in the body. As with laxative abuse, taking diuretics can have no real effect on body weight because when the person takes a drink, his or her fluid balance returns to what it was previously.

The misuse of diuretics can lead to painful swelling throughout the body, which may make people with anorexia think they are fat. The swelling is particularly noticeable in the fingers and ankles. Reduced levels of potassium in the body can make the legs ache and throb and feel very weak on walking.

Misuse of emetics

It is rare for people with anorexia to misuse emetics, but it does occur. Emetics are pills that cause vomiting, so they may be misused as a weight-loss technique. The pills work by introducing an irritant to the stomach, which is why they make a person sick. However, repeated swallowing of irritants may lead to damage of the stomach and even more severe complications such as a heart attack or stroke.

Behaviour focused on reducing the effects of ingested food

Excessive exercise and activity

Some people with anorexia openly exercise to excess, but for the majority this behaviour is more covert. They may start with a gentle programme, but it quickly becomes a dominant factor in their lives. Before long they are spending many hours running, swimming, cycling, participating in aerobics classes and following exercise videos at home. It's not uncommon for them to set their alarms for the early hours of the morning so they can get up and exercise for an hour or so.

People with anorexia try to stay on the move. They are likely to start walking to school or work instead of driving or accepting a lift, and they may volunteer to run errands and make themselves generally useful so they are dashing about and regularly running up and down the stairs. Sitting still and relaxing becomes foreign to them. In fact, when they are forced to wait a long time in a queue, for example, they can become highly agitated and imagine calories transforming into fat. Physical activity soon comes to dominate their day.

Some parents encourage their child to exercise, particularly if competitive sport is involved and the parents are keen for their child to do well. This may cause the parents to miss the initial weight loss and not realize that their child's underlying attitude has changed.

In some cases, people with anorexia hide their obsession with exercise, realizing that carrying out everyday activities won't draw attention to them. However, these activities may include frequently running upstairs, taking the dog for a walk several times a day, standing up all the time, sitting on the edge of their seat and offering to do the shopping, the cleaning, the cooking and so on. They may even keep their bedroom windows open, have very few covers on their beds and wear thin clothing around the house so their bodies will burn up more calories in trying to keep warm.

Despite feeling weak and dizzy from burning too much energy, people with anorexia feel compelled to carry on exercising. Each time they give in to the urge to exercise they are feeding the obsession, which in turn strengthens the need to do it. They are no longer in control of their actions and need someone to help them to stop. They are also putting extra strain on a heart that is already weakened by starvation. Their joints, too, are in danger of being damaged. Because their bones are demineralizing, they are more prone to being fractured. Spontaneous fractures can occur following even light exercise.

Clothes

It's common for a person with anorexia to wear several layers of baggy, often dull, unflattering clothes – generally long skirts or trousers with three or more loose tops and pullovers. She can't contemplate making the most of her appearance because she believes she's a lost cause – at least until she achieves her aim and becomes thin. Unfortunately, that's a journey never to be reached in her mind. Swimming costumes are impossible to consider. Because she's so thin and malnourished, a person with anorexia usually feels the cold, which is one reason she wears layers. Whether the baggy clothing is also intended to hide her shape and to conceal the fact that she's very thin is a question for debate but is usually the case, such is her lack of self-esteem.

Multi-impulsive behaviour

Increasingly, anorexia, like bulimia nervosa, is becoming associated with addictive and self-damaging behaviour, known as multi-impulsive behaviour. This behaviour may include abusing alcohol, drugs and other substances, and unwise sexual activity. The individual with anorexia will view these behaviours as being 'out-of-control' and may describe them as having the same function, that is to quash emotions.

Multi-impulsive behaviour is often reciprocal, in other words one behaviour dominates and the others are recessive. For example, a young man with anorexia may develop alcohol abuse, during which the eating disorder becomes more quiescent.

In addition to being felt as out-of-control, multi-impulsive behaviour is associated with low self-esteem, and very marked depression and anger.

Alcohol and drug abuse

Eating disorders and substance abuse disorders (including abuse of alcohol and drugs) often exist side-by-side, but the mechanism is not understood. Some experts believe that both disorders are manifestations of a common shared underlying cause or set of causes; others that the two disorders may share the same risk factors. In addition, it is theorized that eating disorders and substance abuse disorders are manifestations of a predisposition towards being impulsive. This is thought to relate to the opioid compounds that occur naturally in the body and act like opiates in specific circumstances.

The relationship works in both directions – i.e. just as alcohol and substance abuse may occur in anorexia, so eating disorders are common in women with alcoholism in particular. In fact, figures as high as 30 per cent have been quoted. Of these, one-third were diagnosed with anorexia nervosa and two-thirds with bulimia nervosa. The eating disorder usually precedes the alcohol abuse.

Self-harm

Self-damaging behaviour in the form of cutting, scratching or burning arises in about half of all individuals with anorexia. Cutting is the most common form of self-mutilation and is generally carried out on the arms, legs or breasts with a pin, knife or razor blade. Some cuts are no more than scratches, but the individual may pick at them so they don't heal easily. Other cuts are so severe that they require several stitches, but the person may remove these on returning home. Self-harmers may burn their limbs or breasts with a lit cigarette, or bang their heads or fists against a wall, causing cuts and bruises that are explained away in credible tales. In women, the most pernicious forms of self-damage are cuts and stabbings to the vagina, usually internally. Although light cuts in the area are sometimes used as a means of fabricating a 'period', more usually it's an indication of profound psychological illness. Fortunately, this behaviour is rare.

Self-mutilation may seem like a cry for attention. However, individuals invariably try to cover their scars or burns with long sleeves and trousers. Some self-harmers feel numb or dead inside and report that the action of cutting (or scratching or burning) is triggered by a desperate need to feel something – even physical pain. Other self-harmers are aware of a build-up of tension so great that they feel they would explode if they didn't do something. On carrying out the cut, scratch or burn, the self-harmer experiences a rush of endorphins (the hormones that generate a feel-good factor) which effectively release all tension and stress – at least for a moment or two.

Overdosing

Most overdoses are impulsive and not thought through. Certainly most people with anorexia do not wish to die. It is more a means of indicating to others how desperate and depressed they are feeling. Most commonly, compounds containing aspirin or paracetamol are used, both of which have significant side-effects when taken in excess. Paracetamol in particular can lead to liver and kidney damage, even death.

Risky sexual behaviour

Most people with anorexia lack libido or sexual drive. This is because their weight is below the threshold necessary for sexual hormone activity and hence sexual awareness. Some bulimic anorectics, however, are at a higher weight and so are sexually aware, though they lack the maturity to handle it. This sometimes leads to a young woman unwittingly putting herself in an unwise situation. This is not promiscuity. It stems from low self-esteem and the person's inability to value herself or her body. The sexual activity is seen as punitive and pleasureless, and may be preceded by consumption of a lot of alcohol.

Anorexia, addictive and self-damaging behaviour are all visible symptoms of underlying problems that serve to protect the individual from real difficulties that he or she cannot handle. Giving up this pernicious form of anorexia is particularly difficult, for in so doing, the individual feels defenceless against troubles of which he or she is not fully aware.

4

The physiological dimension

The psychological dimension of anorexia leads to behavioural changes, which in turn result in physiological change due to malnutrition and emaciation. Some serious and potentially fatal physical complications are linked to anorexia. We have touched on some of these physical complications already; in this chapter we will look at them in more detail.

Appearance

When an individual with anorexia loses more and more weight, her face and body take on an emaciated appearance and her bones start to protrude. Her skin becomes dry and tough and fine body hair grows (see the section on 'Temperature regulation' on page 28). Her skin takes on a yellowish tinge, her palms can turn quite orange, her lips become broken and cracked and her hair and nails become dry and brittle.

If she suffers from bulimic anorexia nervosa, she is likely to have swelling (oedema) in her fingers and legs, and puffiness in the face. This is caused by the low levels of salts in the blood that result from repeated vomiting.

Low body weight

The degree of weight loss experienced by individuals with anorexia varies. Usually, weight is lost in a step-wise fashion. Most people with anorexia welcome weight loss and deny anything is amiss. They rarely have a target in mind; however, most feel comfortable below 42 kg. The main female hormones stop their cyclical activity below this weight in most women. With this, adult feelings, including sexual drive, become quiescent. Most individuals with anorexia stabilize at around about 39–40 kg (just below 7 st). Unfortunately, some cannot stop and their weight continues to fall to very dangerous levels.

Not all people with anorexia are emaciated. Some are able to maintain a body weight slightly below normal by not taking the condition to extremes. However, a BMI of less than 17.5 is one criterion in the diagnosis of anorexia (see Chapter 1). A thin physical appearance is often one of the first indications that a person is suffering from anorexia.

Temperature regulation

The body's temperature control system is located in the hypothalamus at the base of the brain. When the metabolic rate is reduced, it is liable to reset itself, causing heightened sensitivity to cold. Hormonal changes and loss of body fat are also contributory factors. A person with anorexia may feel the cold so intensely that she becomes hypothermic at times. People with anorexia grow a light downy hair called lanugo, particularly on the chest and back. It is believed this is a primitive survival mechanism, for the hairs trap air, helping to maintain heat in the absence of the normal layer of body fat under the skin.

The reproductive system

In a girl or woman of reproductive age, even a small amount of weight loss – say 5 kg – can lead to irregular menstruation. If more weight is lost, her periods are likely to stop, a condition known as amenorrhoea. Her periods often fail to return until her body weight has stabilized at normal levels for many months, sometimes as long as a year. Irregular menstruation is often the first physical sign of anorexia.

Another complication in girls and women with anorexia is shrinkage of the uterus and ovaries, and the development of small ovarian cysts known as multi-follicular cysts. These are produced by the ovum (egg) not being released from the ovary into the fallopian tube. Ovarian cysts are associated with a degree of sub-fertility. However, fertility can be restored in women who return to a normal weight.

Hormonal changes usually occur rapidly with weight loss, causing the aforementioned physical effects. Follicle-stimulating hormone (the hormone that releases the follicle into the fallopian tube) and luteinizing hormone (which prepares the uterus to receive the ovum) both cease their cyclical activity. With this the periods stop and sexual feelings become quiescent.

In the unlikely event that the woman becomes pregnant, there is an increased risk of miscarriage, for a starving body finds it far from easy to sustain two lives. If a pregnancy goes to term and a live birth results, the undernourished baby may be very small. (See Chapter 7 for more information on fertility and pregnancy.)

Metabolism

When the body is undernourished, as in anorexia, the rate of weight loss slows down. The body adapts to what it imagines are 'famine conditions' by slowing the metabolism and burning calories at a slower pace. As a result, growth rate is restricted.

Mineral deficiencies

In anorexia, the body can become deficient in essential minerals. In particular, calcium loss from the bones can lead to the development of osteopenia, where the bones break more easily. The more serious osteoporosis – a disease where the bones become even more brittle – may also develop. These are silent conditions that give no indication of their presence until a fracture occurs. Stress fractures caused by impact are particularly likely in those who exercise or over-exercise.

In a recent study, a group of women in their mid-twenties with anorexia were tested for osteopenia and 92 per cent were found to have evidence of demineralization in their spine or hips. Of these, a quarter also had osteoporosis in the spine and 16 per cent had osteoporosis in the hip. Unfortunately, once osteopenia and osteoporosis become established, the demineralization appears to be permanent even when weight returns to a normal range. Sometimes doctors prescribe the 'pill' to replace the female hormones which lay the bone down, or calcium or vitamins. Little or no benefit occurs.

Other mineral deficiencies can cause the following:

- A shortfall in potassium levels can lead to heart problems, for potassium helps to regulate the heart beat.
- A shortfall in magnesium levels can produce muscle tremors.
- A shortfall in sodium levels can cause dangerously low blood pressure and severe dehydration.

Lack of growth

Malnutrition can cause a child to stop growing. In their teens malnourished children just look younger than their age, but in adulthood they can be very short, and an unusual elfin appearance evolves.

Fortunately, in many cases, eating normally can enable children with anorexia to reach their full growth potential. A child may even seem to shoot up while being treated in an eating disorders unit. There are many more, however, who don't catch up fully, despite treatment and complete recovery.

Muscle weakness

With weight loss, the body of a person with anorexia initially turns to its fat reserves for sustenance. When the fat reserves are used up, the body will make use of what little food it gets, and will then begin to break down the muscles for fuel. In extreme cases, this can even include heart muscle, causing the heart to be less efficient at pumping blood around the body.

Muscle wastage can make climbing stairs very difficult. Getting up from a squatting position and doing any lifting can be too strenuous as well. This difficulty is used by doctors as a test for the severity of muscle wasting. If a person with anorexia is unable to get up from a squatting position or falls awkwardly to the side, he or she should urgently be put on a re-feeding programme.

The immune system

In people who are starving, the ability of the immune system to defend the body against viral and bacterial attack can be impaired. On the face of it you would therefore expect someone with anorexia to be more likely to catch colds and flu, and other infections – but, in fact, the reverse is the case. People with anorexia rarely have colds and flu. The reason, however, is probably behavioural, for they avoid social situations and are therefore less likely to become exposed to infection. Some research has suggested that with minor degrees of weight loss, there are beneficial changes to the immune system which might be protective – but this is unproven. What is clear is that with emaciation, an impaired immune system will slow down many aspects of healing, such as that of cuts and bruises.

The organs

The brain

As starvation continues, the brain can start to shrink. The body tries to maintain its function by taking amino acids that would normally form vital proteins. The result is that other tissues within the body are weakened. The spaces within the brain become enlarged, a phenomenon whose significance is currently being investigated.

The heart

In the advanced stages of starvation, the heart becomes weak and its ability to pump blood around the body decreases. Blood pressure gradually drops, causing dizziness and faintness. Indeed, the heart muscle can become so weak that it struggles to function effectively, giving rise to chest pains and palpitations.

One of the more serious problems caused by repeated vomiting is the risk of sudden death from a heart attack. Our hearts require a finely tuned level of potassium and sodium to enable their rhythmical beating. However, vomiting (and also laxative abuse) causes the loss of large amounts of potassium, thus disrupting the heartbeat. A heart attack will occur if potassium levels drop too low. For this reason, it is vital that children who make themselves vomit are admitted to a hospital. Their potassium levels should be monitored frequently and, of course, they should be stopped from vomiting. In adults too, the practice is dangerous. A doctor will carry out an electrocardiogram (ECG) – a test of the heart which shows its electrical conductivity. If an interval called the Q–T becomes lengthened, it is a sign that there may be a problem.

Stomach and gut

Repeated bingeing and purging can give rise to severe heartburn – a burning sensation in the chest. Heartburn is caused when stomach acids force themselves up into the oesophagus, a situation known as acid reflux. Recurrent vomiting can cause stomach acids to erode the teeth and create a sore throat. Gastric juices produced by eating have no food to digest (it's been vomited back) and erode the stomach wall, sometimes producing stomach ulcers. Repeated vomiting can also lead to hiatus hernia. The vomiting 'stretches' the diaphragm (the muscle used for breathing and which separates the abdomen from the thorax or chest). The upper part of the stomach moves, or herniates, through into the chest. This can lead to bleeding and can be pre-cancerous.

When a body is starved, the person will have the feeling of being full when only small amounts of food and drink have been consumed. The reduced enzyme activity caused by starvation also means that of the little food eaten, not all of it is absorbed into the system correctly.

Constipation is another common problem in anorexia. It can give rise to severe abdominal pain as well as discomfort on going to the toilet. 'Faecal impaction' may rarely occur too, in which digested material is trapped in the bowel and cannot be excreted in the normal way. It has to be removed by a doctor or nurse.

Kidney function

The starvation that comes with anorexia can cause blood pressure to be low, and this can result in poor kidney function. Persistent dehydration – where the body is short of water, as occurs in starvation – will eventually damage the kidneys. When laxatives are misused and vomiting frequent, low levels of potassium in the blood can cause impairment of the kidneys.

Are the health problems reversible?

The human body is capable of rejuvenation, regeneration and repair. In other words, given the right conditions, it can heal itself. Good nutrition is the most vital factor contributing to good physical health, for it allows our cells – the smallest but most important components in our bodies – to be nourished continually and washed clean of waste. It also allows the reversal of the many problems caused by starvation. Indeed, when people with anorexia return to their correct weight for their age, sex and height, the majority of the damage caused by anorexia is slowly repaired.

There are three exceptions however. Bone demineralization is unlikely to improve and the consequent risk of fractures remains. Unfortunately a girl who has never started her periods may not menstruate even as she returns to a normal weight in her twenties. (On the other hand, a girl or woman who has started her periods, then stopped as a result of anorexia, is likely to return to a normal cycle.) Dental damage is also irreversible. Teeth may need a great deal of work to look good again.

5

The causes of anorexia

There are as many causes of anorexia as there are people with anorexia. For each individual there is a unique blend of underlying and precipitating factors that prompt the urgent need to lose weight. The seeds of anorexia usually occur in the two to three years following bodily development and the onset of menstruation. It is difficulties with these changes, coupled with problems in understanding and accepting the transition into adulthood, that are at the bedrock of the disorder. More factors must then be thrown into the mix, however, for the condition to develop. These can include personal, family and social events. In this chapter many of these factors will be explored.

Adolescence and individual identity

Adolescence is a period of transition, when individuals develop their personalities and opinions, and gain new experiences from new behaviours. Adolescents are keen to be seen as people in their own right and not just as a part of the family group. It is important to them that their opinions and beliefs are taken seriously – whether they be about politics, moral and ethical values, youth culture or careers – and these are liable to cause family clashes, which may be intense.

Conflicts of some sort frequently occur between parents and their adolescent children. They form the basis of the maturational process as the child becomes an adult. For example, adolescents are frequently under pressure from their parents to take a particular college course that the parents (and not the child) favour. There may be arguments about coming home early at night or having a body piercing.

There are however a small number of children who, as they approach adolescence, have no wish to be seen as individuals distinct from their parents – and from their mothers in particular. These children find the changes and implications of adolescence frightening; they prefer to stay as they are, in a pre-pubescent state, or if puberty has started, they desire to revert to childhood. Weight loss is a way of achieving this. First they lose their newly developing shape; secondly their periods stop and sexual drive ceases; thirdly, they have no desire to join their peers in the newly discovered adolescent world. They retreat, as it were, into a psychological and physiological childhood.

No parent wishes this to happen to a child, but in some circumstances a parent may gain covertly. If the parental marriage is under strain, the child's illness will tend initially to bring the parents together. More perversely, one parent may blame another for the illness. A child terrified by the adult world, where a seemingly permanent 'safe' structure like the family is ruptured by emotions they cannot understand, will wish to retreat from it.

In an alternative scenario the future adolescent anorectic becomes deeply resentful and feels that she must take control of her life. She may severely restrict her food intake – especially in families where meals are fundamental to family life. Causing her parents to be concerned and anxious gives her a feeling of power, allowing her to impose her will.

The attention gained by a refusal to eat can also be sought in other situations. For example, an adolescent in the shadow of an older sibling who is perhaps excellent at sport or who wins prizes for her paintings can feel an intense need to be 'seen' within the family. Developing an abnormal eating pattern can draw attention – and negative attention is seen as being better than no attention at all.

Twins, in particular, can have a difficult time in adolescence, for they not only have to develop independence from their parents, they also need to become separate entities from each other while still related. An interesting study was carried out a few years ago into the difficulties faced by identical twins. The study indicated that some mothers idealize the state of twin-ship, seeing no need to make their identical twins individuals in their own right. Indeed, some twins are unable to live apart from each other, but also feel unable to live close, comparable lives. Out of such turmoil, anorexia can spring.

Low self-esteem

All people with anorexia have low self-esteem – although how it manifests varies. Some authorities argue that it is a learned behaviour passed on from parents, whereas others hotly disagree. Undoubtedly, though, an unwise comment can hurt many years afterwards. For instance, a parent may suggest that her daughter could do with losing weight or may regularly comment on how slim and pretty her cousin is. Such remarks are common, and most recipients don't develop anorexia, but a girl to whom they are addressed may feel unattractive and inferior. She will begin to equate a particular weight and shape with success.

Supporters of the learned behaviour theory would give another example: that of a mother with a low opinion of herself who may dress unattractively and make derogatory remarks about her own size and shape, which her child then transposes on to her impression of herself.

Low self-esteem often results in the person being overly self-critical, particularly in adolescence when looks take on so much importance. Losing weight gives her a boost and feelings of achievement – and those feelings are so good that they can drive the girl to seek contentment in extremes.

Body-image problems

Linked to low self-esteem is a poor body image. In the West, children are becoming preoccupied with their appearance at younger and younger ages and are more likely than ever to develop a poor body image. It doesn't help that their contemporaries are frequently on diets and that everyone is striving to improve their looks.

Children like to copy each other – it's the way they feel they fit in with the crowd. Some of those predisposed to developing anorexia may have always felt on the outside of things; they start to diet because the others are doing it and because they believe that if they are thinner they may be accepted by the 'popular' girls. To their surprise, they find they can actually stick to the diet better than the others, which attracts both praise and envy. As a result, they experience heady feelings of power and success, perhaps for the first time in their lives. Consequently, they throw themselves into the diet with even more gusto.

Body-image problems are often first recognized by parents when they see their child 'mirror-gazing'. Most people would accept that it is reasonable to look in the mirror to check one's dress or apply make-up. The individual with anorexia, however, stares long and hard at each body part, concentrating on thighs, hips and bottom, which are pinched and pummelled. She loathes and detests her shape – particularly if it has brought unwanted sexual attention. In general, however, it is not sexual attention that is troubling. Rather, there is a general disturbance – a recognition that the quiet, secure life of childhood has gone for ever and cannot be reclaimed.

Body image and society

Throughout history the fashionable body shape has changed significantly. In the seventeenth century Rubens painted the well-rounded female forms that society then admired. Hourglass figures were contrived by extensive corsetry in the late nineteenth century, while curvaceous figures were more obviously displayed by the Hollywood actresses of the 1950s. Their large breasts and big bottoms, offset by slender waists and shapely legs, were quite different from the ultra-slender forms of Jean Shrimpton and Twiggy in the early 1960s. This change from the well fed to the emaciated was reflected in other 'commodities' at that time. Cars and refrigerators also became smaller and more compact, which emphasizes how women's bodies were seen as commodities and viewed in quite a different way from men's.

The female, in all mammals, is fattier than the male. Cats are fattier than toms, and dogs more muscular than bitches. A healthy woman is also fattier than a man, but there is a difference between the fatness of a woman and that of other female mammals. Women are the only mammal in which the fat is differentially distributed, being concentrated particularly on the thighs, the buttocks and the breasts. There is no physiological reason why the fatness of a breast should be sculpted under the nipple and milk sacs. The fat can be anywhere on the body and be just as effectively available. But while in most other mammals initial sexual attraction is based on smell, this emphasis on shape means that initial sexual attractiveness in humans is based on vision: the male is drawn to the female figure. The underlying issues of weight and shape are therefore rooted in core aspects of femininity and human sexuality.

Interestingly, there is no evidence to support the notion that any particular body shape or size is more appealing to men than any other shape. Furthermore, there is no evidence that men are drawn to women who are very slim. When one asks for a personal opinion from a variety of men, there's a wide disparity in their preferences. Some men like slim women, but generally they prefer a fuller figure. Certainly, not many admit to being drawn to bony, angular women.

In truth, there is no evidence that men are drawn to any particular shape or weight in their partners. There is, however, evidence that women prefer women to be slim.

Media influence

The female shape that is idealized by the media today is very slim with slender limbs, a 'washboard' stomach and C or D cup breasts. Images of today's embodiment of perfection are everywhere we look – in magazines, television, advertising and elsewhere – and the majority of us feel lacking in comparison. Indeed, in a survey, teenage girls and boys reported that very slim or muscular models tended to make them feel insecure about themselves.

Advertising companies have made people feel that they can remodel themselves at will, resculpting their bodies with 'wonder' creams, ridding themselves of acne with 'miracle' face washes and giving themselves gleaming hair with amazing hair-care products. Moreover, in women's magazines, the latest diet crazes are discussed in great detail, the people they have worked for offering gleaming testimonies that can only spur the reader into trying them out.

On television we are exposed to female presenters who are immaculately turned out. The presenters selected for our screens are mostly 'ideal' specimens of womanhood, but you don't see the armies of professionals working behind the scenes to make sure they look good. Some viewers might believe that this is how they look in reality, in their everyday lives. It all adds up to an overall picture of perfect people with perfect lives – a picture that couldn't be more false, yet is the benchmark for so many. People who already have low self-esteem may think that they can never match up, so they feel like failures and their self-esteem drops further.

If one looks at the most popular magazines on the newspaper racks, the images on the covers represent approximately 0.3 per cent of the population, leaving a massive 99.7 per cent with no chance of measuring up. One must remember that looking good is a career for these people. Many have fitness trainers and nutrition advisers; plenty have even undergone cosmetic surgery to correct their 'faults'. And of course, there is then the airbrush to make lumps, bumps and blemishes disappear completely.

In the Western world, the average fashion model is 5ft 11in tall and weighs 54 kg (8½ st), while the average woman is 5ft 4in tall and weighs 63 kg (10 st). Fashion models are thinner and lighter than 98 per cent of the remainder of the female population. In the UK, even the average shop mannequin is clad in a size eight or ten. It is no wonder then that women are dissatisfied with their size and shape.

It doesn't help that today's eternal promotion of the ideal shape and look sends the message to women in particular that they must be appealing on the outside to be valued by others. This can lead them to believe that the way they look is central to their happiness and success in life. Surely it is unfair that the media have such power, that they have the ability to generate a negative body image, lack of self-esteem and general unhappiness? Yet it is we, the consumers, who allow them that power. We allow them to sell us the message 'thin is in' many times a day, and through numerous avenues.

Social pressures

Social pressures, created by media influence, can cause an individual to feel even worse about herself, for it seems that today only slender people can be part of the 'in crowd', or be judged as acceptable in everyday society. Throughout history there has been pressure to fit in, appearance-wise – but in today's world of television, internet and glossy publications, the pressure to fit in is emphasized a thousand-fold. Indeed, it has been estimated that today's young woman sees more images of beautiful women in one day than her mother saw throughout her entire adolescence. It's no wonder, then, that many modern young women yearn to be like their ideal images, that they tend to think there are more beautiful people in society than there actually are.

Powerful unconscious associations can be made by body size and shape and this can lead the adult with anorexia into worrying relationships. For instance, a woman with anorexia may represent a 'little girl' or even a 'little boy' figure, being dependent and biddable in a childlike way that satisfies a prurient sexual drive in her partner. That she is childlike, yet legally an adult woman, can provide her partner with a perverse incentive to collude with her anorexia.

Early feeding problems and habits

The family meal is increasingly an institution of the past. Picking and grazing at food is common today, with children noting and learning their parents' eating habits. Poor eating habits, however, do not automatically lead to anorexia. It's common for people with anorexia to report 'faddy' eating in childhood and early adolescence – yet the overwhelming majority of faddy eaters don't develop anorexia. Of more concern is the use of food as a means of communication. Food given as a reward or food removed as a punishment may lead to inappropriate associations. For instance, a child may perceive emotion in terms of food. If food is given when the child is anxious or angry, these emotions in later life are likely to lead her to seek out food. That said, the association between early misuse of food and anorexia has not yet been clearly established.

In general, women with anorexia make good mothers. They tend to worry, however, that their habits might be passed on to their children, particularly to daughters. There is good reason for this concern and many mothers with anorexia make a determined effort to rid themselves of their disorder if their daughters are nearing puberty. They believe that in some way the condition might be 'catching'.

Childhood trauma

A number of years ago it was felt that anorexia might be a direct result of abuse, particularly sexual abuse. Indeed, a high incidence of sexual abuse was reported in people with anorexia. More careful studies over the years have shown this not to be the case, and it has been seen that sexual, physical and emotional abuse is higher in all neurotic disorders occurring in women. Women who are depressed or who have anxiety disorders are more likely than the general population to report abuse, though it must be emphasized that the incidence is still low. The prevalence of sexual abuse is nevertheless fairly consistent across all neurotic disorders, including anorexia. In people with anorexia who report sexual abuse, their condition is likely to lead to the multi-impulsive clinical picture that combines addictive and self-damaging behaviour with the misuse of food (see Chapter 3).

Other childhood traumas that have been put forward as causative factors include bullying, accidents or life-threatening illnesses. However, there is little evidence to support these theories. In fact, they often stem from speaking to individuals rather than objectively assessing a large number of people with anorexia. Such childhood traumas are common and only in some children does anorexia supervene.

Genetic predisposition

Recently research has indicated that some people may be genetically predisposed to developing anorexia. However, it's difficult to assess whether a particular behaviour is induced more by nature or nurture – this meaning the relative importance of a person's innate qualities (nature) versus her personal experiences (nurture) in determining or causing behaviour.

It is likely that an individual inherits a gene that makes that person vulnerable to anorexia, which then develops under particular conditions. These conditions could include growing up in a household with a relative suffering from an eating disorder, and being exposed for example to the attention the relative receives due to their illness, the constant emphasis on food, weight and shape, or the apparent rewards for achieving a low weight.

Risk factors that contribute to the development of anorexia

- low self-esteem
- perfectionism
- family dieting
- an eating disorder in the family
- parental marital problems
- critical comments, for example regarding shape and size
- adverse parenting
- depression in the family
- drugs or alcohol abuse in the family
- family obesity
- an early first menstrual period
- anxiety disorders
- sexual abuse
- media pressure to be slim

6

Signs to watch out for

Most parents, friends and partners initially ignore the obvious signs of anorexia. But when suspicion is raised, what do you look for?

If you are a parent in particular, it's incredibly scary to think that your child has anorexia. However, recognizing the condition is an important turning point, for it's only when you have the truth that you can begin to do something about it. The following tell-tale signs may indicate that your child has anorexia:

- She is losing weight rapidly.
- She tries to hide her weight loss instead of being openly proud of her dieting achievement.
- She restricts her food intake or avoids meals.
- She becomes anxious around meal times.
- She is preoccupied with her weight and may weigh herself numerous times a day.
- She counts calories and knows the calorific values of all the foods she eats.
- She says she's trying to eat healthily but does it by eliminating many foods, including most standard carbohydrate foods. Fats are also cut out.
- She becomes vegetarian, or even vegan.
- She appears to be eating well, but the food on her plate is very low calorie.
- She's not happy with her body shape and size.
- She has a distorted view of her shape and size, believing herself to be overweight and full of lumps and bumps.

- She denies being hungry.
- She makes excuses to avoid eating.
- You find hidden food – items she has claimed to have eaten.
- Large quantities of food go missing at times.
- She starts without apparent reason to cook her own food.
- She takes up strenuous physical exercise.
- She becomes more active in general, despite looking tired and gaunt.
- She appears quite depressed, smiling far less often.
- She becomes antisocial, avoiding family celebrations and not wanting to go out with her old friends. She appears quite withdrawn and isolated in her life.
- She wears many layers of clothing.
- She becomes perfectionist and immaculately tidy, perhaps producing flawless handwriting, very rounded and small. Everything must be exemplary.
- Her behaviour regresses: she may return to having tantrums. Such behaviour should be viewed as an indication of anguish and unhappiness.
- She disappears to the bathroom after meals to make herself sick. The room may smell of vomitus for a time afterwards, as may she herself.
- She begins using laxatives, for which the evidence may be obvious; or you notice a lot of laxatives or diuretics in a cupboard or drawer.
- She begins lying about what she's eaten.
- She disappears to her bedroom after meals to exercise.

Physical signs

In addition to these behavioural signs, there will probably be physical indications that something is wrong:

- Her skin may become dry and her hair may be thinner.
- She may have an 'ill' appearance.

- There may be puffiness of the face and fingers.
- She may develop the fine bodily hair known as 'lanugo'.
- Her gums may bleed and her teeth start to erode.
- There may be small swellings in the parotid glands, just in front of her ears. (Over time, the swellings become hard.)
- There may be small swellings beneath and around the jaw (swollen salivary glands).
- If she makes herself sick as a purgative, there may be grazes on her forefinger knuckle, where her fingers scrape against her front teeth. She may even have a chronic blister on her forefinger knuckle where it rubs against the upper teeth (Russell's sign).
- She may sleep poorly and particularly wake early.
- She may be constipated and her stomach bloated.
- She may feel the cold.
- She may lack energy and experience muscular weakness.
- She may suffer bouts of dizziness.
- Her menstrual periods are likely to become hit and miss, or even stop altogether. This is a sign that the condition has reached a dangerous stage and that the diet is out of control.

Weighings

When monitoring your child's weight loss, never base any decision on one weighing. If you are concerned about your child's weight, it is more accurate to measure her weight twice a week. Try to use the same scales and be confident that they're properly calibrated. If in doubt, cross-check by comparing the home scales with a pharmacy weighing machine. Always weigh at the same time in the day. It's best done before breakfast and at least six hours after drinking. Plot your child's weight on a graph using one centimetre for a kilogram on the vertical scale and one centimetre to represent a week on the horizontal line. Keep the graph as a record and show it to your doctor.

Body mass index

Learn to be comfortable with using BMI, which corrects for height and is a much more accurate way to assess the severity of anorexia than simply weighing. BMI is explained further in the section on 'Recommended weight' in Chapter 9 (page 87). The normal range is 20 to 25. For a formal diagnosis of anorexia the BMI must be less than 17.5, although anyone with a BMI below 18 should see their GP. Below 15, there is medical concern and below 13, admission to hospital is usually required.

Signs that admission to hospital may be necessary

Admission to hospital should be considered if:

- the person isn't benefiting from outpatient treatment;
- the person is becoming very frightened;
- there are signs of dehydration, such as refusal to drink, or because of vomiting or laxative abuse;
- vomiting is persistent and regular, whether the person is underweight or not;
- there are symptoms of poor blood circulation, such as low blood pressure and a slow pulse;
- the person has severe depression.

7

Fertility and pregnancy

Anorexia predominantly strikes during adolescence and early adulthood. These are normally a woman's most fertile years, and as a result of extreme weight loss she may not start her menstrual periods or they may suddenly cease. This means she is unlikely to become pregnant and give birth to a healthy baby. The absence of menstrual periods (amenorrhoea) strongly suggests that a woman isn't ovulating, that is, her ovaries do not release an ovum or egg each month. In plain language she is temporarily infertile, and for some it can become a permanent condition.

The longer a woman has had anorexia, the greater her risk of facing fertility problems of some kind. Having said that, approximately 80 per cent of women who manage to overcome their anorexia regain their ability to conceive. Indeed, their periods may automatically start up when they begin to put on weight. It's not advisable to get pregnant, however, until you are well on the road to recovery, or feel fully recovered. Women who get pregnant while struggling with anorexia can find the physical and emotional demands overwhelming. They not only risk seriously damaging their own health, but also that of the unborn child.

Pregnancy exerts an enormous strain on any woman's body, for as the foetus develops it takes nourishment from the mother. A pregnant woman with anorexia may find her already scant reserves seriously depleted, causing her to experience exhaustion and depression. If she manages to bring the pregnancy to full term, she may then lack the energy required to meet the demands of a newborn child and her health may deteriorate further.

Any woman with an eating disorder should delay pregnancy until she is healthy.

Anorexia and fertility

Low body fat percentage

When a woman's body fat percentage drops below a certain level, her body fails to produce the levels of hormones necessary to stimulate ovulation. Moreover, rapid weight loss combined with malnourishment forces her body into a state of emergency, making it more concerned with survival than being equipped to have a baby.

As well as hormonal imbalances, vitamin and mineral deficiencies can result from anorexia, making it even more difficult for a woman to conceive.

Accidental conception

Despite their low body weight, some women with anorexia are able to conceive. Some, and particularly those of Asian background, may ovulate and menstruate even at quite low weights. Others may not yet have had a first period, but if sexual intercourse takes place shortly after the first egg is released, it can be fertilized. It's also common for a woman with anorexia to ovulate sporadically and not always be aware that she's hit a fertile patch.

It can be risky, therefore, to think you are unable to conceive because you have never had a period, or because your periods stopped some time ago. For these reasons, if you don't want to get pregnant, you should always use protection when making love.

Miscarriage and other risks

In a study of the relationship between anorexia and ovulatory infertility (the failure of the follicle to ripen and discharge an egg), significantly more women with anorexia were found to have miscarried than healthy women. Miscarriage in anorexia generally occurs because the woman's body is not capable of carrying a baby to full term, the body rejecting it as a result.

Women with anorexia who are pregnant are more likely to have a termination of pregnancy. This may be because there was a complication with the pregnancy, problems with the foetus were detected early or the woman felt emotionally unable to cope with the projected weight gain and upcoming responsibility.

As well as miscarriage, anorexia in pregnancy is related to a greater than normal risk of the following:

- a high risk pregnancy;
- gestational diabetes;
- an increase in damage to the mother's teeth and bones;
- worsening of any other pre-existing condition related to anorexia, such as cardiac or liver damage;
- an incompetent cervix, causing spontaneous abortion;
- placental separation;
- too little amniotic fluid;
- pre-eclampsia;
- other complications during labour, such as a breech presentation;
- necessity for a Caesarean delivery;
- premature delivery.

Some premature babies have neurological and developmental problems well into early adulthood, and possibly longer. Some of the problems include a low IQ, learning disabilities, cerebral palsy and psychiatric illness such as Attention Deficit Hyperactivity Disorder (ADHD). As they reach adulthood, these people can remain dependent, failing to develop effective social skills and successful relationships with other people. Babies of low birth weight may appear to be healthy, but often fail to reach their full expected adult stature. The more premature the baby and the lower its weight, the more likely is the disability.

Problems for the foetus

Research has indicated that a woman's low body weight and food restrictions can cause a multitude of problems for the developing foetus. To conserve energy, the foetus may decrease its rate of metabolism – which can lead to obesity, heart disease and diabetes later in life. The woman's dieting can also cause scarce nutrients to be directed to the foetal brain, leaving inadequate amounts to be sent to other vital organs such as the liver and kidneys. These organs may then not function effectively when the baby is born. The baby is also at risk of the following:

- delayed foetal growth;
- jaundice;
- raised possibility of death in the last trimester of pregnancy or within one month of the birth;
- stillbirth;
- low birth weight;
- low Apgar scores – the Apgar score is a reading of the baby's skin colour, heart rate, movement, breathing and reflexes, taken very soon after the birth;
- birth defects such as cleft palate and cleft lip;
- respiratory distress immediately after birth;
- major disability, such as blindness, mental retardation and cerebral palsy.

Considering motherhood?

If you are trying to decide whether or not to have a baby and have a history of an eating disorder, it's important that you are aware of the pitfalls as well as the joy and fulfilment a child can bring. Having a baby will not provide the motivation you need to recover, so please don't think that. Pregnancy and motherhood carry with them a great deal of stress and responsibility, and you need to be in a healthy place in your life before even considering getting pregnant. Some women become pregnant because they are desperate to be loved by someone. However, it's your love, protection, strength and good health a baby will desperately need. You don't need a baby, but a baby will need you.

If you are not yet fully recovered from anorexia and wondering whether or not to get pregnant, ask yourself the following questions:

- How comfortable will you feel with the changes in your body during and after the pregnancy? Will your feelings set your recovery back? Will they make your anorexia worse?
- Are you confident that you will take good care of your body and the baby during and after the pregnancy?
- Will you be able to handle the stress of a shrieking baby when you're not sure why the baby is crying?
- Will you be able to cope with the responsibility of a little human being who is entirely dependent on you for its health and wellbeing?
- Are you certain you will be able to encourage your child to eat normally?
- Are you strong enough in your mind that you will reach out for help if you need it?
- Are you willing to face the possibility that you may pass your eating disorder on to your child?
- Will you be able to cope with any postnatal depression? (It can be mild to severe.)

Of course, no one can tell you whether or not you should get pregnant. The decision has to be yours, in the end. However, please be aware that you may not be ready at the moment, and that a few more months and a little more counselling can make all the difference to your physical and emotional success as a mother.

Improving your chances

If you have a history of anorexia and wish to conceive, there are things you can do to improve your chances. Your main aim should be to recover from anorexia before you start trying to get pregnant – if you are not regularly replenishing your resources as the baby is developing inside you, you could find yourself at very low ebb physically and emotionally.

The following guidelines should also help:

- Maintain a normal body weight for at least six months before trying to get pregnant.
- Ensure that you continue to eat a healthy diet.
- Avoid any bulimic behaviour, such as bingeing and making yourself vomit.

Counselling

Before you try to get pregnant, it's recommended that you ask your doctor to refer you for skilled counselling – motherhood is stressful and you may be tempted to revert to your old behaviour once the baby is born. Counselling can teach you invaluable techniques that help you to cope with the stress.

Fertility testing

If you are on the road to recovery, or have recovered from anorexia and are having trouble getting pregnant, it's advisable that you visit your doctor. He or she may decide to refer you for fertility testing. There are currently several available procedures that can help a woman to conceive.

Pregnancy and birth

If you have had – or still have – anorexia and are now pregnant, you need to take extra special care. For example, sufficient calcium intake is important during pregnancy as your teeth and bones might become weak – the baby's need for calcium takes precedence over yours. If calcium is not replaced by dairy products, dark green leafy vegetables and other sources, you could suffer broken bones and stress fractures in years to come.

- Tell your doctor about your anorexia to ensure you get the best possible prenatal care.
- Ensure that you take your prenatal vitamins, and ask your doctor whether you need iron or calcium supplements.
- Eat a healthy diet and allow yourself to put on as much weight as you need to during each trimester.
- Don't miss any prenatal visits.
- Don't enrol in a prenatal exercise class unless your doctor recommends it. In general, you should not over-exert yourself.
- If you start to feel uneasy about your body and the weight you are gaining, don't hesitate to talk to your doctor or counsellor.
- If lingering body image issues are bothering you, seek help from your doctor or counsellor.
- Taking classes on pregnancy, childbirth and child development can reassure you about what to expect.

Binge-eating and pregnancy

If binges are a part of your illness, these will become less frequent as your pregnancy proceeds. As your baby grows, it will become impossible to eat large amounts of food. However, binge-eating tends to return with a vengeance after the birth and particularly during weaning. It's best to ensure that you have treatment in the latter stages of your pregnancy. Some of the techniques described in Chapter 9 will help.

The emotional aspect of pregnancy

A woman who has had anorexia or is still struggling to overcome it can be elated to find she is pregnant – she had possibly assumed she would never be able to conceive. She may continue to be thrilled about the little life growing inside her, but start obsessing about all the weight she knows she has to gain. She is likely also to worry excessively about how quickly she will be able to lose the weight after the birth.

To have a healthy child, a pregnant woman should gain between 11 and 16 kg (25–35 lb). However, the idea that it is necessary to put on so much weight can strike horror into the heart of someone with a history of anorexia. It's like telling a normal woman that she has to gain 100 pounds. With each pound a pregnant anorectic gains, she becomes a little more frantic and a little more depressed. Indeed, a small number of women feel so out of control that they try to harm themselves or the unborn child.

Some women get pregnant because they believe themselves free of anorexia and feel they can cope. It's unfortunate, though, that pregnancy can bring back all those difficult thoughts about weight, all those bad habits related to diet. Pregnancy is an extremely emotional time and is ten times harder for a woman recovering from anorexia.

It's important, therefore, that the medical professionals involved with your pregnancy know your history. They can then ensure that you are taken good care of and receive the appropriate counselling, which should help you to cope. With proper care, you can overcome your eating disorder and give birth to a healthy child.

You should also make sure you receive proper help and guidance after the birth, particularly when it comes to losing your postpartum weight safely.

Pregnant women with anorexia or recovering from the condition can be especially sensitive to other people's comments.

Remarks such as 'You're looking really big', or 'Is that all baby, or are you eating a lot, too?' can be very upsetting. It's best to avoid saying anything about the woman's size, for even comments such as, 'Are you worried about losing the weight?' and 'How much weight have you gained?' can provoke extreme anxiety.

Some women with anorexia view pregnancy as a welcome break from their worries over weight. They know that having a baby is an important business and are able to set aside their anxieties in favour of their child's health. Other women fall into a black pit of depression when their tummies begin to swell. They can't see that the weight gain is an essential part of producing a healthy child, and that much of the additional weight is actually baby. These women are liable to continue to starve themselves and may even lose weight instead of gaining it.

Fortunately, most women fall between these extremes.

After the birth

After the birth of your baby, it's important that you continue to eat regular, nutritious meals. You will need to keep up your strength to be able to cope with the many changes and demands brought by your baby, and to handle any postnatal depression. If you are breastfeeding, you need to eat well to ensure you produce sufficient milk and so that you don't pass any vitamin deficiencies through your milk to the baby.

Motherhood for women with a history of anorexia

The demands of motherhood take a great physical and emotional toll on a woman, causing high levels of stress at times. You may believe yourself fully recovered from anorexia, but the demands can be such that you find yourself falling back into your old habits of starving, perhaps using occasional binge/ purge behaviour. If you have received skilled treatment at an eating disorders unit (as either an in-patient or out-patient), or been counselled by a qualified therapist, you will have learned how to cope when you feel overwhelmed. Now is the time to use these techniques. If, however, you received no such counselling, it's never too late to get help. Go to your doctor, explain your situation and ask for a referral to an eating disorders expert.

Don't be a poor role model

Unfortunately, a woman with a history of anorexia can be a poor role model for her child where food, eating, weight and body image are concerned. For example, she might underfeed her child to ensure that she's slim, or overfeed her to prove to the world (and herself) that she is a nurturing parent. As the child grows older, the family may be plagued by power struggles over food and eating. A daughter is at risk of developing an eating disorder of her own, and a son may believe that a woman's weight and shape are her most important assets.

Help your child to develop a positive body image

It is always wise to remember that you are a role model for your children, and as such you should take care over how you behave and what you say and do. Instead of dieting, you would be advised to follow a long-term healthy eating and exercise programme, of the type you would like your children to respect and copy.

In order to help your child to develop a positive body image and relate to food in a healthy way, follow these important steps:

- Show your child that you love and value her. A warm hug from a parent is worth more to a child than any toy or treat.
- Compliment your child on her particular talents, accomplishments, values and efforts.
- Examine your dreams and ambitions for your child. Make certain you are not stressing looks and slimness as a way she might attain her goals.

- Make sure your child knows she can come to you with any problems she has. Ask her about her day and be interested in her life.

- Avoid giving both sons and daughters the message that girls are less important than boys. For example, don't let boys off doing housework and shopping.

- Watch television with your children and discuss the images you see. Explain that the beautiful people in the media make up only a tiny proportion of the population and that the average adult is a little overweight, with less than perfect looks.

- Consider the way you see your own body and how this has been shaped by media images and prejudice against weight. Discuss the ugliness of prejudice with your child and help her to understand that we all have a different genetic make-up that gives a diversity of body shapes and sizes.

- Try to accept yourself as you are. Daughters listen to the way their mothers talk about themselves and each other in order to learn the language of womanhood. They can only learn to love and accept their bodies if they see women who love and accept their own.

- Make sure your child understands that weight gain is a normal part of development, and that girls in particular put on normal fat tissue at puberty.

- Let your child make her own decisions about food. If you are concerned that she is not eating enough of a certain food group, try not to be. Just make sure that nutritious food and snacks are always available. Children tend to sort themselves out, diet-wise, in the end.

- Try to measure people by what they say and do, not by how they look. Your child will follow your example.

- Teach your child by example that eating a variety of foods in well-balanced meals, three times a day, is good for health.

- Learn all you can about the dangers of dieting and discuss this with your child.

- Avoid making negative statements about food, weight, body size and shape.
- Don't ever make overeating a reason for exercise.
- Perform a little gentle exercise every day for the buzz it gives and the knowledge that it is making your body stronger and more supple.
- Don't avoid an activity – swimming, for example – because the clothing required draws attention to your shape and size.

8

Treatment

If you have anorexia and would like to be free of it, the recovery process entails gaining weight. This is by far the greatest psychological hurdle and can cause a great deal of panic. Try not to dwell on the need for weight gain, however, but think about the things that you will be able to do when your life is no longer dominated by food.

If you are the parent of a child you suspect has anorexia and she is not gaining weight, or is sticking at the same low weight, it's important that she sees the family GP. It's not advisable to strong-arm her to the surgery, however – in all likelihood she will only feel resentful and resist all efforts to be helped. Unless she is dangerously underweight – in which case she should be hospitalized immediately – she needs to accept for herself that she has anorexia and that it needs to be treated. You can help her to do this by explaining the many health risks linked to anorexia. You can also make it clear that anorexia is a psychological disorder, that it very cleverly makes her think she can't live without it and is driving her further and further away from the person she really is, taking over her identity and making her think that she will be nothing without it. Explain to her that it may seem that anorexia is her friend – maybe she feels quite emotionally isolated and anorexia is the only companionship she feels she has – but the hard truth is that anorexia is an enemy, not a friend. Seeing anorexia as an unfriendly entity is essential to the recovery process.

It's also important to assure her that you will support her throughout the duration of the treatment regime, and even after that.

Starting the recovery process

An individual with anorexia is likely to feel very afraid of the whole treatment process, particularly as it involves gaining weight and challenging her entire belief system regarding her weight and relationship with food. She may feel ambivalent about embarking on recovery and contemplating giving up the illness that has become part of her identity. She will also find it difficult to acknowledge that she's underweight – perhaps even dangerously underweight.

If you have anorexia, confiding in someone close who you trust will want to help – whether it is a parent, carer, partner or a friend – is a positive step towards recovery. Moreover, speaking openly of your problems helps you to face up to them and see what's happening in a more detached light. You could ask your confidante whether they will accompany you to your GP to give you moral support. It's likely they'll be only too happy to go with you. Not only that, they'll probably be keen to support you as you proceed through the recovery process.

Seek treatment early

That treatment is sought as early as possible is essential to the recovery process, particularly for young children in whom starvation is accelerated. Furthermore, an individual in the early stages of anorexia is likely to recover quickly and fairly smoothly. A person with anorexia of up to four years' duration will need more intensive therapy. It is an unfortunate fact, though, that treatment may be delayed. This is because individuals are generally strongly opposed to acknowledging that there's a problem and that they need help. When a person has suffered from anorexia for over four years, the condition is more deeply entrenched and therefore more difficult to treat. This does not mean the condition is past being treated. It means simply that treatment must be more intensive and prolonged.

Treatment alliance

During your treatment you will work with many professionals who will all support you in your fight against your eating issue. It is important to remember that you are all fighting against the same thing, not battling with each other. It may seem hard at times to work with the team, especially when you are being asked to do difficult things (and the eating disorder is fighting back). However, try to keep in mind that treatment guidelines are there for a reason and are designed to help your recovery. All the professionals work together as part of a team, sharing information with each other to make sure your treatment is appropriate to your needs. For example, an occupational thera-pist will help you to identify ways to improve your quality of life and living skills; a dietician will provide information about meal requirements and nutritional advice; a clinical psycholo-gist will offer counselling and psychotherapy on an individual and/or group basis; specialist nurses will offer practical assist-ance (such as preparing food and going on shopping trips) and emotional help (such as exploring feelings, managing impulses to use unhealthy food behaviours and building self-esteem); a psychiatrist will oversee your treatment and prescribe medica-tion if necessary.

Managing your feelings

During your treatment, you will get much more out of it if you try to open up about issues that provoke a lot of anxiety. Being able to discuss such things will make you more aware of your feel-ings. However, as the resultant emotions may be overwhelming and unpleasant, the team will help you to manage them. You will be able to talk about your feelings to your 'named nurse' (or key worker) on a regular basis, but as feelings can surface at any time, you will be encouraged to ask for time to speak. The team realize that people with anorexia often struggle to feel that they are worthy of other people's attention and find it difficult to ask for time. However, when you can manage to do so, it's another step forward. You are recognizing that you need help and gaining the necessary skills for getting it.

Out-patient management of anorexia

In anorexia of a fairly short duration, your family GP might try to manage it within the practice. If so, he or she will assign a nurse to weigh you on a weekly basis, advise you on good nutrition and give you an idea of what you should be eating. The nurse may also educate you on basic health issues and provide information about appropriate local resources, including the local anorexia self-help group. The latter may give out information packs, provide a monthly newsletter and loan out relevant books. Speaking to people who are experiencing (or have experienced and have come out the other side) the same problems can be extremely beneficial, too.

At the same time, the GP might encourage you to speak about any problems you have. If you still fail to put on weight, or stay at the same low weight, the GP will refer you for psychological treatment by a specialist service. The purpose of such treatment is to promote weight gain and healthy eating, reduce health risks and the symptoms related to anorexia, and make both psychological and physical recovery possible.

Community mental health teams

The first step to accessing more specialized treatment is for your GP to refer you to a community mental health team (CMHT). This is a team that manages people with a variety of problems and is headed by a psychiatrist and includes nurses, psychologists, occupational therapists and psychotherapists. You are likely to be seen on an out-patient basis in your local area and will be assigned to a key worker who will coordinate your care. If your difficulties do not improve, your local services may feel you need more support and/or input from a specialist service and you may be referred to a specialist eating disorder service for out-patient treatment.

Specialist out-patient treatment for anorexia

The majority of people with anorexia are treated on an out-patient basis, which is less disruptive to a person's life than day- or in-patient treatment. Out-patient treatment can be any of the psychological treatments outlined later in this chapter, and may be delivered by a clinical psychologist or a specialist nurse.

Once the eating disorders unit has received your referral, you will be assessed by an out-patient team member who will ask about your problems with eating and aspects of your personal history too. It may be difficult and exposing to speak of these things, but it's necessary information in planning your treatment. During psychological treatment, your progress will be monitored and if you do not make significant improvement, you are likely to be referred for day care or in-patient treatment. Except for individuals with severe emaciation, most will only be considered for in-patient or day-patient treatment when the appropriate out-patient treatment has not been successful, or in cases of anticipated suicide attempts or significant self-harm. If, on being assessed, you are deemed as being at moderate to high risk of severe health consequences, in-patient treatment will be considered for you.

If you are referred to an eating disorders unit, it will be the one nearest to your home so as to allow the easy involvement of your family or carers. This will also enable you to maintain contact with friends, as well as school, college or work, and will make for an easy transition between primary and secondary care services. Sometimes, though, you or your advisors may suggest one of the national eating disorders centres.

Treatment philosophy

The treatment team at an eating disorder service believe that every person has intrinsic worth and is deserving of dignity and respect. They recognize that each of their patients has the potential to move forward and will do their utmost to enable that to happen. However, the individual is responsible for making changes. The treatment team can offer information, motivation and support but the change has to come from within – you have to want to get better. It is hoped that a trusting relationship will develop between you and the team, which should help you to talk about difficulties you are facing along the way. Any inclusion of and sharing of information with families and significant others will only take place with your consent.

Such teams operate an equal opportunities policy towards their patients. This helps to ensure that all patients are treated individually, and that their differences are acknowledged and respected. Although treatment is tailored to the individual, it is necessary that there are universal boundaries and guidelines within any eating disorders setting when treatment takes place in a group, or in a day or in-patient unit. You are likely to be very scared and the eating disorder will fight to carry on with what it was doing before. There are certain expectations within treatment (such as eating three meals a day) and these are there to take away the anxiety that comes with decision making and having to give yourself permission to eat.

Day-patient treatment

If you are referred for specialist treatment, you will be required to attend the unit on a regular basis as a day-patient. Programmes vary but attendance is usually required on four to five days a week. Day-patient treatment programmes generally comprise therapy (individual, group and family), dietary advice, education and group activities. There is likely to be one or more communal meals, as well as practical advice on shopping and food preparation. The staff will support you to eat in a way that is considered 'normal' in order to help re-establish a more healthy relationship with food, for example you would be discouraged from 'spoiling' food by over-using condiments or from cutting food up into tiny pieces.

Although day-patient care can be a useful alternative to in-patient treatment, some people receive day-patient treatment after an in-patient stay in order to get used to spending time at home again after being in hospital. The transition from having to eat all meals as an in-patient, then being at home and having to feed yourself again, often makes people feel very anxious. The process of integrating back into the community is liable to be more difficult than you imagined and day care provides extra help and support from your key nurse, peer groups, your chosen self-help group and the community you live in.

Unfortunately, not everybody is able to work within a day hospital programme. Some people may require more intensive treatment in an in-patient unit. Also, some people will be admitted as in-patients following unsuccessful out-patient treatment if there is no day hospital in the area.

In-patient treatment

In-patient treatment is likely to be considered in the following circumstances:

- if you have a BMI of below 13.5;
- if your weight loss was fairly rapid;
- if your physical condition is poor;
- if your thought processes have become very rigid;
- if you have a health condition in addition to anorexia – e.g. diabetes;
- if there is a further psychological dimension – e.g. depression, self-harm, overdosing, obsessive-compulsive disorder, bulimic behaviour.

Intensive treatment at an eating disorders unit will generally last for a few months. It is only resorted to in severe cases, as it can cause a person to connect more strongly with 'being ill' and reduce her sense of control. Feeling out of control is terrifying for people with anorexia and they seek to regain a sense of control by restricting their food intake further. As a result the person may become more determined to resist treatment or may lose weight once more on being discharged.

In-patient naso-gastric re-feeding

If you refuse to eat normal foods when your weight is dangerously low, staff at the unit must take decisive action and either feed you intravenously or by a tube into your stomach via your nose. You will continue to be encouraged to return to a normal diet, in the form of smallish, regular meals that get you used to eating again.

If you are refusing to eat or refuse to have a naso-gastric tube placed into your stomach, the team may assess you for compulsory treatment under the Mental Health Act. This would only be considered as a last resort, due to the importance placed on the treatment alliance between the individual and the team, and the need for a person to want to get better in order to beat the illness. However, when the risks of physical damage (and even death) are this great, there is no time for further negotiation. When people are seriously unwell and malnourished, they may be sent to a medical hospital to be re-fed on a ward where their physical status can be monitored. They can then return to the eating disorder service to engage in psychological treatment, when it is safe to do so.

Target weight

During your treatment, the treatment team will set a target weight. See page 87 for details of how this is done. A woman will, in most cases, function normally at this weight, her hormone levels returning to normal and her periods reappearing. At less than this weight, her body may fail to function normally. A man's target weight will be set at the average weight for his age, sex and height, as boys have a lower percentage of body fat. The National Institute of Clinical Excellence (NICE) recommends rates of weight gain of 0.5–1 kg per week in in-patient settings, and 0.5 kg per week in out-patient settings.

You will be expected, after a few days, to gradually increase your calorie intake until you are able to gain a steady 1 kg per week. As weight is gained, you should notice that your metabolism is faster and that you feel far less fatigued. You will probably be kept occupied and supported by staff and your peers after eating so you are less likely to dwell on the amount of calories you have consumed, and have little time to vomit or burn off the calories through excessive exercise.

Many individuals with anorexia fail to accept that they need to achieve their given target weight. Indeed, they have already decided on a target weight that is lighter than the thinnest person they know. Being told the weight they are expected to reach can fill them with panic and dread, causing them to fight with the staff team. However, the team understand the importance of holding firm boundaries and how shifting the goal posts will make it more difficult for someone to come to terms with the prospect of gaining weight.

Often, people with anorexia will try to maintain their weight just below their target weight; however, recovery is not possible without reaching target weight. Psychologically, target weight is very difficult to reach, as some individuals believe that other people will think that they are now 'well' again because they have made physical progress. The team recognize, though, that there is much work still to do at this point, and once target weight is reached, the emphasis can be shifted to tackling underlying issues rather than weight.

Treatment approaches

Psychological interventions offered by eating disorder services exist within the framework of a model that focuses on how thoughts, feelings and behaviour are all related and influence one another. This framework encourages each individual to examine and change how they think so as to bring about changes in how they feel and act. Treatment is offered on both a group and individual basis. At the beginning of individual treatment, the therapist will work with you to understand what factors are contributing to your difficulties and make an individualized 'formulation' or idea of what's going on. This formulation is used to plan treatment and identify goals.

More specifically, treatment interventions you may be offered include motivational work, psychodynamic therapy, dialectical behaviour therapy (DBT), 'standard' cognitive-behavioural therapy (CBT), and schema-focused CBT. These psychotherapies can be delivered on an individual or group basis, and in in-patient, day-patient or out-patient settings.

Motivational work

Motivational work is essential when working with people with anorexia, given their attachment to their symptoms and reluctance to give them up. The treatment team will work with you to look at the function that anorexia has served for you and why it is so hard to stop using the behaviours. While this is usually a starting point in therapy, given the fluctuating nature of motivation, it is revisited throughout treatment.

Psychodynamic therapy

This form of psychotherapy offers an opportunity to explore in depth the emotional issues underlying your eating disorder. It will focus on how your relationships, both past and present, have contributed to your current situation, and will help you explore how the relationships you have developed during treatment (either with other patients, or with professionals involved in your care) might reflect other relationships that have been problematic. The aim of psychodynamic therapy will be to help you make connections between the past and the present, in order to help you understand the part you play in your relationships, and enable you to gain insight into your behaviour and identify where you might want to make changes. This can be delivered in group or individual settings.

Dialectical behaviour therapy

DBT combines the basic strategies of behaviour therapy with eastern mindfulness practice. It was originally developed for chronically suicidal individuals but has since evolved into treatment for binge eating, other impulsive behaviours and personality disorder. DBT is most appropriate when the main trigger or maintaining factor for the eating behaviours is difficulty in regulating emotions. The components that are particularly useful are mindfulness (being aware of thoughts and actions that are happening in the present moment), distress tolerance and emotion regulation.

Family therapy

Family therapy can be another component of treatment and can be conducted on an in-patient, day-patient or out-patient basis. It is particularly effective when the disorder has been present for less than three years and when treating children. Family therapy is often conducted in a room with a one-way mirror, enabling the session to be observed by a second party. This means that two therapists can see complicated family dynamics more clearly and from different perspectives. They can then work out together with the family how to tackle problem areas more effectively. It is also a chance for family members to be involved and to say how things are for them – to bring any issues within the family out into the open. It is a useful way to look at how family members interact with each other and how this relates to the anorexia. Unfortunately, suspicion often shrouds the prospect of family therapy, family members wrongly assuming that they are viewed as the root cause of the problem. It is no doubt of benefit for family problems to be openly discussed, as they can contribute to anorexia and make recovery more difficult. However, therapists are aware that the condition is seldom caused by poor parenting or difficulties within the family.

Family therapy can also help your family to support you through the recovery process. Family members may be with you at mealtimes and so on, so they are best placed to assist. When a family is united in the task of feeding and caring for a person with anorexia, there is far less chance of a relapse occurring. Members of any kind of committed relationship, such as a partner or a supportive best friend, can be invited to attend family therapy.

Standard cognitive-behavioural therapy

This treatment approach involves identifying unhealthy links between eating behaviours and beliefs about eating, shape and weight, and the challenging of those beliefs through performing behavioural experiments and confronting thought patterns. It helps you to recognize that certain thinking patterns provide a distorted picture of what's going on in your life, giving rise to anxiety, depression and anger. During CBT sessions, you will work together to identify the 'truths' that form the foundation of your entire belief system, which is generally based on feelings not facts. For instance, you may have an instinctive feeling that you're overweight, that you're unlovable in your present form, and that everyone is staring at you in disgust. These self-defeating thoughts are generally automatic and may never have been explored or challenged. CBT encourages you to assess the evidence for your beliefs. The therapist will help you to re-evaluate your beliefs so you can base the foundations of your life on what is real.

CBT involves doing homework tasks outside of therapy sessions in order to continue to test the assumptions that are driving the eating disorder. For example, someone may avoid eating chocolate bars because they think that eating one bar will cause them to gain 5 kg. If they are able to actually eat a chocolate bar and do not change anything else they are doing, they will see that one chocolate bar is not sufficient to cause them to gain 5 kg. In addition, CBT aims to educate you about food and eating, weight and shape, and to eliminate many of the myths about dieting. It will help you to recognize and deal with potential triggers of your anorectic behaviour and, if there has been a slight downward slide, will show you how to get back on track.

Schema-focused cognitive-behavioural therapy

This approach is similar in nature to conventional CBT, but involves addressing a more complex level of thoughts often relating to an individual's early experiences (those about the self as defective, a failure), rather than beliefs about eating, shape and weight. Schema-focused CBT tends to be most appropriate for those patients with more complex co-occurring conditions, including personality disorder.

Antidepressants

Antidepressants can be of benefit to many people with anorexia, whether they are receiving treatment or trying to help themselves. They can enable people who binge-eat or obsess about their appearance to do so with far less intensity and frequency. However, antidepressants cannot stop these behaviours altogether. Neither can they be effective on their own as treatment of anorexia – psychotherapy, counselling and re-feeding is required, too.

The drugs currently being prescribed for people with anorexia are

- tricyclic antidepressants such as imipramine, desipramine and amitriptyline
- monoamine oxidase inhibitors such as phenelzine
- selective serotonin re-uptake inhibitors (SSRIs) such as flu-oxetine and fluvoxamine.

Nowadays, SSRIs are usually prescribed first for anorexia. If one antidepressant should fail to be of benefit, your doctor or psy-chiatrist will be able to prescribe another.

When your doctor or psychiatrist recommends an anti-depressant, she or he will discuss the side-effects. Because many people with anorexia have weakened blood supply to the heart and other vital organs, the side-effects of these drugs can be pro-nounced. If antidepressants are decided upon, cardiac function should be monitored regularly by means of ECG.

Group treatment

Attending group sessions during your day-care or in-patient stay can help you to achieve your admission goals. Some groups are centred on an activity, such as painting, card-making or com-puter skills, while others focus on feelings. Speaking in a group situation can provoke anxiety, but this can be worked through within the group and with your named nurse. Learning to be assertive and say what you mean will benefit your relationships and all areas of your life, especially when you leave the unit. Some groups can be attended from early on in your treatment, but others are more relevant in the later stages, i.e. when you have reached target weight and are starting to maintain your weight at a healthy level.

Individual in-patient or day-care unit programmes may vary,

but are likely to contain groups centred on some of the following themes:

Living skills

This group provides a safe environment in which you are free to express yourself and explore any practical difficulties you have related to maintaining your weight, while learning various coping strategies and life skills to help you maintain a safe weight.

These life skills include the following:

- goal setting
- time management
- leisure planning
- money management
- support systems
- welfare rights
- stress management
- discharge planning.

Meal cookery

The aim of this type of group is to enable you to prepare appropriate meals that allow you to maintain a safe weight. In this group you will be engaged in planning meals for yourself, shopping for the ingredients, preparing the meal and finally eating it. These tasks are performed with the support and encouragement of a team member. In addition, the group functions as a support group in which you can voice your concerns or feelings about emotional or practical issues.

'Creative' and 'lifestyle'

This group focuses alternately on creative and lifestyle activities. The creative option allows you to participate in self-directed creative activities (such as needlework and craftwork) that you find enjoyable. As a result of your achievement and positive feedback from the group, your self-esteem should improve and your quality of life be enhanced.

When the group is engaged in lifestyle activities such as written, verbal or creative exercises, fellow support and feedback can raise your motivation to have a positive lifestyle.

Art therapy

In an art therapy group you will be encouraged to express your thoughts and feelings as freely as possible through your artwork. No skill or experience at all is required. The point is not to produce a pretty picture, but to allow the expression of certain feelings that are difficult to articulate in words. It should help you also to get in touch with feelings that are buried deeper than words, and of which you may not even be aware. When the time for painting or drawing is finished, the group members will help each other to understand their artwork. There may be nuances within it that offer understanding of your emotions. You will then be better prepared to change.

Psychodrama

You may be invited to join a psychodrama group. During the session, one patient is selected to work on her chosen problem area, such as a troubled relationship or difficult feelings in relation to her weight. Other patients in the group help by taking on significant roles – a partner, parent or boss, for example. They might even play the patient herself. Throughout the session, various scenes are enacted, culminating in the group sharing their thoughts and impressions with the individual. For the individual to know that others share the same feelings and fears is helpful; it is also of benefit for other group members to identify with the scenarios played out. Again, you gain an understanding of yourself which can assist change.

Group psychotherapy

Here you are encouraged to bring any problematic feelings or experiences into the group in order to share and explore them with others. A safe, confidential space is created in which you can examine the relationships between yourself and your fellow patients.

Anger management

Disordered eating behaviours serve to suppress difficult emotions, so when those behaviours are no longer being used, the emotions return. This group helps patients to express and deal with their anger more effectively.

Body awareness

Once you have reached your target weight, you may join a body awareness group. The aim of this group is to increase your awareness of your body and explore your current perceptions of it when you are at a healthy weight. Topics such as what influences the way we feel about our bodies, sexuality, outside pressures, media portrayals of women and so on are covered.

Exercise

Most units run an exercise group, in which the theory of health, fitness and exercise is discussed. After the theory, physical exercise and group activities are carried out, at an appropriate intensity. The occasional ball game and a little walking or swimming will not undo the benefits gained from your increased calorie intake. So long as you are gaining the required amount of weight, a little exercise does no harm. In fact, it is important that patients re-establish a healthy relationship with exercise, especially if they have used it to compensate for eating in the past.

Harm reduction in-patient care

Sometimes people feel that they are not yet ready to tackle the process of recovery but want to make smaller changes in their lives. Harm reduction programmes aim to help you address certain aspects of your anorexia, such as the way it inhibits you and makes you feel sad. It is not about conquering your anorexia, but about making it more bearable and improving your quality of life.

If you decide that a short-stay admission is right for you at the time, it is likely that an out-patient nurse will work with you to determine your admission goals, diet, length of stay and the groups you will attend. Before you come into the unit, the problems you would like to work on and the length of your stay will be established.

Harm reduction treatment usually requires a brief admission for a few weeks. Your first week of admission will be an assessment period during which you will meet all the team staff and make a joint decision about whether short-stay care is best for you at that particular time – some individuals may respond better at a later date. If you agree to be admitted, your admission plans will be finalized, with the help of the team. Your care will then be reviewed on a weekly basis, usually during the ward round (a meeting of team members involved in your care). If you have particular issues you would like to discuss, it may be best to write them down beforehand to help you remember and reduce anxiety.

When you come to be discharged, all the people involved in your care will join you in looking at what you have achieved. With your input, your ongoing needs will be discussed and a plan to meet them put together.

Short-stay admission plan

With guidance, you will set goals that are focused on improving your problem areas. For example, you may want to learn how to do the following:

- eat regular meals with all the major food groups, including fat;
- buy and prepare food;
- reduce your unhealthy behaviour around food, such as performing rituals and eating alone;
- gain a little weight and learn how to maintain it.

If gaining weight is not part of your admission plan, you will be expected to maintain your current 'holding weight'. You can discuss this with the team dietician and liaison nurses before you are admitted to the unit.

If you abuse alcohol, are socially isolated and so on, the team will aim to help you make it less of a problem. However, food and weight issues will be the primary concern.

In-patient treatment of children

In-patient treatment of children under 12 with severe anorexia may take place, first of all, in a hospital paediatric ward. The child may require rehydrating (by means of a saline drip) and intravenous feeding (through a tube inserted into a vein) for a few days to stabilize her symptoms. However, there will be no treatment for her psychological problems here, and the nursing staff are not trained in anorexia care. It is advisable, therefore, that she is quickly referred to a specialist eating disorders unit where the staff have a great deal of experience in treating anorexia.

Educational needs

In assessing whether a child should have in-patient care, her educational and social needs are weighed against the need for urgency in treatment, for example in cases of severe emaciation. Schooling is particularly important and missing several months of it can cause a child to fall behind the rest of the class. Moreover, missing school is often distressing for a child with anorexia as such children tend to want to do well. In some cases, however, the danger to the child's health and wellbeing must take precedence and she must be admitted for in-patient treatment. The child's teachers should be able to let her have a certain amount of schoolwork to do at the unit.

Men with anorexia

As discussed in Chapter 1, men can suffer with anorexia (or bulimia), although a much smaller number actually receive treatment. This is thought to be because professionals are less likely to detect and diagnose men's problems around food, attributing them to other causes. Another barrier is men's reluctance to acknowledge that they have an eating disorder and to seek help, perhaps due to the stigma and shame that sufferers feel around anorexia. Men are also less likely to seek help for emotional difficulties in general.

For men with anorexia or bulimia, the symptoms are often similar to those experienced by women with these disorders. There are some differences, though. For example, men are less likely than women to misuse laxatives or make themselves vomit, and are more likely to exercise excessively to counteract the effects of eating. It is also thought that men are more likely to binge-eat instead of restricting their food in response to feeling negative about their body image. Studies have shown that weight, shape and body image are also important to males. In one survey, a third of the boys questioned stated that they needed to lose weight and had tried to diet an average of four times.

If you are a man who thinks you are suffering from anorexia, it is important to seek help. The pathway to treatment is the same as that outlined above and the same treatment options are available to you. If you receive day-patient or in-patient treatment, it is likely that you will be treated alongside girls and women who are experiencing similar problems. Being the only male in a predominantly female environment (both of peers and staff) is not ideal. However, at low weights, men and women have more similarities than differences. Therefore, men with eating disorders face the same issues and will still benefit from the same treatment as women with eating disorders.

9

Helping yourself

The earlier anorexia is recognized, the better are the chances of successful treatment and recovery. Delay in recognition can cause the disorder to become more severe and deep-seated, and recovery to be difficult and protracted. Often the hardest part is accepting the problem and acknowledging that you need help. Anorexia may have been a part of your life for many years but only now are you able to think about doing anything about it. People with anorexia can be particularly opposed to accepting that anything is amiss. However, forcing a person to have treatment rarely works – you have to want to get better.

The fact that you are reading this book shows you are at least contemplating changing your eating patterns and lifestyle, but you may be undecided as to whether you are ready to face this yet. The recovery process is likely to be the most difficult task you have ever taken on and things may get worse before getting better. At the same time, whether occasional relapses occur or not, it will be the best thing you have done in your life. Before you begin your new venture, try to follow these important steps:

- No time will seem 'right' to start to change, so make a commitment to start immediately. And stick to it, no matter what! Every time you feel afraid and consider lapsing into the familiar pattern, remind yourself that your anorexia will no longer be in control of you – you yourself will be in charge again.

- Make a realistic mental picture of where you would like to end up when you are free of your problem. How did you want your life to be before anorexia got in the way? Now visualize how to get on to that path and see yourself doing so in the near future.

- Now visualize how you would like yourself to be. What qualities and traits would you like to show? Try as hard as you can to see yourself that way.
- Keeping a diary will be enormously helpful, for you need to record your use of the techniques you are about to learn. Use a new notebook, buying one today if you don't have one. By the time the notebook is full, you will be a long way on the road to recovery.

Read through the whole of this chapter before following the instructions. Then you can always go back to it whenever you need a reminder. If something doesn't go to plan, don't feel you have failed and give up on the whole process. You are quite likely to have slip-ups along the way, for your anorexia will not be willing to relinquish the ferocity of its grip. If this happens, just get back to your recovery programme and focus on each small success. People with anorexia often strive for perfection in all areas of their lives, and recovery is no different. However, there is no such thing as a 'perfect' recovery. There will inevitably be setbacks and occasional relapses, but these can be turned around and thought of as learning experiences.

If you have real difficulty following the instructions, you may benefit from seeing a skilled therapist who can lead you sensitively through each process.

Who may not benefit

The self-help instructions in this book are not likely to be appropriate for people in the following categories:

- Those who are fixed into a pattern of grossly disturbed eating habits. If you are willing to try to change, you are not in this category.

- Those who are isolated completely. To gain dominance over anorexia, people who live isolated lives are likely to need the support of a therapist they can see on a regular basis.
- Those with a very low body weight. Individuals with severe malnutrition should first and foremost seek specialist treatment.
- Those who are so depressed they cannot summon the motivation to try to change. Such people should visit their doctor. At a later time, it may then be possible to follow this programme.
- Those for whom anorexia is only a part of a much larger problem. This includes people who self-harm or have serious relationship problems.
- Those with anorexia and a medical condition related to eating, such as diabetes. Such people should seek specialist help.
- Women who are pregnant. Medical help should be sought first of all.

If you belong to one of the above categories, you should speak to your doctor. He or she is the right person to treat you or advise about local specialist care. For everyone else, try to see the programme in this book as a starting point, something you can move on from to specialist treatment, if need be. The latter is always an option, whether you have had such treatment in the past or not.

Your recovery programme

Making a start

The first stage in your recovery programme is to establish exactly where you are now. Take an honest look at your life, then read the following points and write down your thoughts at the back of your new notebook. Be completely honest with yourself. Facing up to the reality of your current situation is an essential part of the recovery process. Your anorexia is likely to have developed as a means of dealing with something unpleasant in your life. The reasons behind the anorexia vary, as do the ways in which people experience anorexia.

- Try to remember what prompted you to try to lose weight in the first place. This is different for all anorexia sufferers and could be due to low self-esteem, or to feeling unable to control other aspects of your life; it might be a way of suppressing difficult feelings or because you feel undeserving of good things. Try to think about what anorexia means for you.
- If you binge, what is it that compels you to do so? How exactly do you feel before, during and after you binge? If you purge, try to pinpoint exactly how that makes you feel. Try to be completely honest with yourself.
- Try to think about when it is that you most struggle with food. Is it when you are feeling a certain way, with certain people or in certain situations?
- If you feel very anxious about your weight and body shape, try to remember what triggered it. Did you experience some kind of trauma? Did you feel unable to speak about this trauma to your family? Were you teased about your appearance at school? Did one particular comment do the damage?

Looking at the pros and cons of living with anorexia

Even if you have decided to try to change your eating behaviour, it is likely that you still have mixed feelings about taking the leap. To help to organize your thoughts and see the situation more clearly, you might find the following helpful:

- Make a list of the advantages gained by your anorexia.
- After you've done that, make a list of the disadvantages.

Do not be surprised if, at this stage, the advantages outweigh the disadvantages, if you are being entirely honest. Otherwise, you would have been able to let go of the anorexia before now. Your anorexia may have been a good friend – but it was a friend who would not give you any peace, who did a lot of damage to your life. Although your anorexia may have protected you from facing difficult feelings and situations, it is likely that it has been detrimental to your health both physically and psychologically in your career, relationships and friendships.

Look a few years ahead

It can be difficult to think about how your life will be without anorexia, especially if it has been part of your identity for a long time. It can also be very scary to think about what will be left once the anorexia has gone. You may have missed out on your adolescence through being unwell and in the childlike state that accompanies anorexia, so the idea of being an adult without anorexia as an identity could be difficult to imagine. One way is to imagine seeing a friend and explaining to her what your life is like now, with the anorexia, what you've been doing and where you've been. Imagine seeing that same friend after a five-year interval and only being able to say that things are still the same, and that food, weight and shape still dominate your life.

Now imagine that after five years, you are seeing the same friend and talking about the joyous, healthy and satisfying life that you are now leading. Any problems that you are struggling with at the moment have been resolved or you have found satisfying ways of coping. Imagine describing in detail how you are spending your time, your relationships, and your perspectives on the past.

It is often when you can project a few years ahead and see how much you have missed out on that you realize how anorexia is holding you back and will continue to do so. Looking ahead is likely to firm your resolve to change.

Weight gain

The first step to regaining your life from anorexia is to embark on a weight gaining regime to promote physical health. This will not only repair some of the damage that the anorexia has done to your body, but will improve your concentration, mood and sleep. Weight gain is difficult to do without support because if you were receiving specialist treatment, you would be given an individualized plan to help you to manage weight gain gradually. However, this section covers some general principles to get you started.

Recommended weight

To determine whether your weight is healthy or not, doctors and dieticians use body mass index (BMI). BMI is calculated by using the following equation: weight (in kilograms) divided by height (in metres) squared. If you have access to the internet, some websites work out the equation for you. (Examples are <www.nhsdirect.nhs.uk/magazine/interactive/bmi/index.aspx> or <www.cdc.gov/nccdphp/dnpa/bmi/index.htm>)

The BMI ranges for young people below 15 years of age are different, as are the ranges for men (due to differences in body composition).

Working out your BMI in this way provides an objective marker of your weight and body shape. Even though you may feel grossly overweight, if your BMI is below 17.5, it is in the anorectic range. If your BMI is below 13.5, you are severely malnourished and should see your doctor so that you can receive hospital treatment.

Because you have a fear of your normal weight, it is not possible, emotionally, for you to calculate your goal or target weight. We will therefore set out a formula that will calculate it for you, using the tables in the Appendix.

First, remember how old you were when your illness began. Add to that age any time when you were in recovery. The best marker of this is (if you're a woman) if your menstruation returned. The sum of these is then the age that you use for this calculation. Thus, as an example, if your current age is 24 but your anorexia began at 16, and you have had two years since then of normal menstruation, your age for this calculation is 18. This method is used because it is unlikely that you would be able to tolerate being at the average weight of a 24-year-old but it is probable that you could accept emotionally being at the average weight of an 18-year-old. This method has the added advantage of linking your target weight to your personal emotional development. The target weight in the example above if your height is 5 ft 5 in would be 56.7 kg (125 lb or 8 st 13 lb) (see page 115).

Remember, you will not be happy with your target weight because of your weight phobia. Remember too, though, that you cannot get well unless you reach this weight. Even 200 g (8 oz) below is insufficient because the reason you are 200 g below is the fear of being at your personal normal weight. Hence, by definition (see Chapter 1), you still have your anorexia.

Reviewing your eating habits

Before changes can be made to the way you eat, it is important that you know exactly what is happening with your eating just now. You can do this by keeping a detailed daily record of when you eat, what you eat, where you eat, whether you felt it was excessive, whether you felt out of control, whether you vomited or took laxatives, and whether you used exercise to burn off the calories. Becoming aware of your eating habits may make you feel worse at first, but to enable you to make essential changes in this area, it is crucial that you know exactly where you are now.

Monitoring charts

To record what you eat, use a full page of your notebook every day. Do not just write down the food you feel OK about having eaten, and do not be afraid to record everything if you feel you have overeaten. It will be a boost to look back on the record when you're eating healthily once more. Write down your thoughts and feelings while you are eating, and afterwards as well. Trying to remember everything at the end of the day will not be as effective, as there will always be things you forget.

Look at the example chart below, and then mark up several pages in your notebook with the date and headings, as shown.

Time	Food and drink	Place	Exercise/vomiting/ laxatives	Thoughts*
8 a.m.	3 cups black coffee	Kitchen	Exercised	Feel fat. Dieting
9.30 a.m.	2 cups black coffee	Kitchen		Must lose weight
12 p.m.	2 cups tea	Kitchen		I'm gross, I can feel the fat
2.30 p.m.	1 mug of soup, glass of water	Kitchen		I don't want to see anyone
5.50 p.m.	Scrambled egg with 1 slice of toast, 1 cup black coffee	Kitchen		Feel I have had too much to eat
9.40 p.m.	Cup of black coffee	Lounge		Depressed. Gross

* You will want to write your thoughts and feelings in more detail than we have shown

Reviewing your monitoring charts

When you have monitored your eating for a week, look at the period as a whole and try to identify any patterns in your eating. These patterns will be particularly evident in people who binge-eat. For instance:

- Is there a time of day when you eat less?
- Is there a particular time when binges are likely to take place?
- Are there times when you can more easily control your eating?

- Are there times when you are more likely to skip meals?
- Are there specific situations that trigger your binges?
- Is there a particular type of food that you eat during binges?
- Are there periods of time when you eat nothing at all?
- Are these periods often followed by binges?
- Are days when you restrict what you eat generally followed by binges?

When you think carefully about your answers to these questions, several things may become evident. For example, it may be clear that you feel less hungry in the morning and early afternoon, and so exist on not much more than black coffee. You may then be ravenous later in the day and tend to feel that you have lost control and over-eaten. This in turn increases the likelihood that you will not eat much the following morning. It is far better to break up your eating throughout the day (see 'Making a meal plan' on page 91) – even if you don't feel hungry in the morning. That way you are less tempted to binge.

Coping with weight gain

In anorexia, the weight gained in the early stages of recovery is made up of a higher proportion of muscle tissue and water than fat. Therefore, although you may panic and feel that you are becoming fat, the weight gain is actually due to increased water retention and muscle, not fat. You may also panic because you feel that you are putting on most of your weight on your stomach. This is mainly because your digestive system is not working well again yet and there is a build-up of liquid and gas in your stomach, making you feel bloated.

You may also be concerned that, once you make a decision to start gaining weight, your weight increases relatively quickly. This is because you were dehydrated before, and you are now retaining water until your body's fluid balance is restored. You may see swelling, particularly in your ankles, but this is not permanent (and again it is water, not fat). By following a meal plan, your weight gain will become more gradual and more predictable.

It may be tempting to weigh yourself every day, or perhaps even several times a day, to keep an eye on your weight. This will only serve to make you more anxious, as small fluctuations on the scales due to fluid will appear magnified. Although it can be difficult, try to weigh yourself just twice a week or arrange to be weighed by someone else, perhaps a nurse at your GP's surgery.

It is also likely that, after eating a meal from your meal plan, you will panic and feel that you have eaten too much. You may be tempted to restrict what you eat at your next meal because you are terrified at what will happen to your weight. At this point it is very important that you do not compensate, as this will only serve to increase your anxiety. If you continue to manipulate your food intake, you will not know how the planned meals are affecting your weight, as you will have too many complicating factors. By tolerating the discomfort, you will find that your weight becomes more predictable. There is more information about anxiety management later in this chapter.

Practical help with food

Making a meal plan

The next stage of the recovery programme entails learning to eat regular meals in a controlled way. This means eating breakfast, lunch and an evening meal, with three snacks in between. Eating regular meals in this way, and abandoning your weight-loss diet and binges, will help your body to find its natural weight – we all have a resting weight to which our bodies naturally return if we don't try to control our weight. After all, our bodies function best when they are in the middle, neither overweight nor underweight.

Many people with anorexia are terrified that if they start eating, they will not be able to stop. However, this controlled meal structure will provide a recommended daily amount of food and will cause you to return to a resting weight where you are able to function at an optimal level. Although people with anorexia are often fearful that they will become bulimic once they start eating, this is only likely if their pattern of eating remains abnormal.

Forming your meal plan

It is important that you eat at set times rather than when you feel hungry or just feel that you need food. When you have been denying yourself food and ignoring feelings of hunger, before long your sensations of hunger or fullness will have become distorted and will not reflect your physical state. Therefore, in the early stages of restructuring your eating, it is helpful to follow a plan of meal and snack times, to help your body reconnect with hunger, and when it needs food.

Look at the sample meal plan and write down the most suitable times for you to have breakfast, dinner and your evening meal. Add to that the times you would prefer to have three snacks. There should be a gap of no more than three or four hours between eating times. These times should then be strictly adhered to – that is, you should make sure that you eat at these times, even if you don't feel particularly hungry. If you postpone your meal, your appetite will increase; if you are a binge-eater, you are likely to want to binge later on.

The following is a sample meal plan:

8.00 a.m.	Breakfast
10.30 a.m.	Snack
1.00 p.m.	Lunch
3.30 p.m.	Snack
6.30 p.m.	Evening meal
9.30 p.m.	Snack

Don't be alarmed by the number of eating times in the plan. Your own plan should be similar, depending on your particular routine. If you feel hungry when you are not supposed to eat, the short period between eating times means you can hearten yourself with the knowledge that you will be able to eat before too long. As you are probably thinking constantly about food, it is also easier to find something to distract yourself with if you only have a couple of hours to fill.

People with anorexia may find it difficult at first to eat five or six times a day. However, this meal structure is vital as it keeps blood sugar levels up and reduces the physiological triggers for bingeing. If you were severely underweight and being treated in hospital, you would be given liquid-like foods at first that are easier to eat to get you used to eating again. Then you would move on to half portions of more balanced meals, which would eventually be increased to full portions. If you are doing this on your own, you might start by eating something at the three meal times, and then build up to adding in snacks and increasing the quantities to the recommended amounts. Although you might find it hard to stick to these times at first, it is important that you build up to this over a few weeks.

It is helpful to treat each meal or snack separately. If one meal or snack does not go to plan, try not to dwell on it but box it off so that you can continue with the rest of the plan. As mentioned previously, many people with eating disorders struggle with perfectionism and if one meal is missed or does not go to plan, they think they may as well write off the rest of the day's meals. However, it is never too late in the day to turn things around.

Guidelines for normal eating

With some effort, food can take a less prominent role in your life again and eating can be a less stressful experience. The following guidelines aim to help you to re-establish healthy eating – they are not rules, so you do not need to follow them rigidly:

- Plan to eat three main meals a day, with adequate carbohydrate (potatoes, pasta and cereals).
- Plan to have up to three snacks each day. This will reduce your hunger pangs and lessen any urge to binge.
- Eat in company, if possible.
- Distract yourself if you are struggling with eating.
- Keep to regular eating times.
- Eat proper breakfast foods at breakfast time (such as cereal, porridge, toast and so on); proper lunch foods at lunch time (sandwiches, beans on toast, baked potato with tuna and so on); and proper evening meal foods at evening meal time (chicken, spaghetti bolognese and so on).
- Plan your meals beforehand so you know exactly what you'll be eating and when you'll be eating it.
- Plan the next day ahead. This should discourage impulsive eating. It also eases the sense of chaos felt by many people with anorexia.
- Before going food shopping, plan all your meals for the next week. Buy only the food you have in your plan, and make sure you have everything you need so you cannot use this to justify skipping meals.
- Identify the times at which you are most likely to have difficulties with food, and then plan to eat with people, use safer foods and so on.
- If you are thinking too much about your weight and shape, it may be because you are anxious or depressed. Try to identify any problems you have and talk them through with someone you trust, rather than turning to anorectic behaviour to manage your feelings.

Try to keep these guidelines in mind as you go through the week. At the end of each week, look at your chart and note any changes in the way you are eating, whether good or bad. Consider how any changes for the better were made and how you can maintain them.

If, after the first week, you have forgotten to write down a lot of what you ate, or could not put into action any of the guidelines for normal eating, don't be discouraged. Simply go back to the beginning and start again. If this seems like a chore, remember that doing this has the potential to turn your life around, enabling you to do things that will make you truly happy again.

Choosing types of food

The food you choose to eat in your meals and snacks at this stage should be food that you can eat without it leading to you wanting to binge, purge or restrict later on in the day. If you are unsure of the amounts you should be eating, watch what the people around you eat, particularly those who are viewed as 'normal' eaters. However, beware of modelling your eating on someone who has their own issues with food, weight and shape.

Some people find it easier to measure their portions out so they know that they are having the same amount each time and that it is what is required. Although this is not ideal in the long term, it may be useful in starting you off with the right quantities. Another method is to buy single portion meals at the supermarket. Your anorexia may rationalize these as unhealthy but, in reality, you want to avoid them because you are fearful of gaining weight.

In order that you are not confused about what exactly to eat, it is essential that you plan your meals in advance, as stated. Write down your plan every evening at the top of the next day's food monitoring sheet. Having a meal plan and sticking to it will help to reduce the anxiety that you may be feeling when faced with giving yourself permission to eat and choosing which foods to have. Having had the decision taken away, people often report that they feel less guilty about eating as it is something that they have to do. You may find this helpful too.

In the early stages of recovery, it may be helpful to stick to 'safe' foods in order to ensure that you keep to the meal structure. Many people with eating disorders find it easier to stick to contained food – for example two pieces of toast and an individual tin of baked beans – so that they do not have to worry excessively about measuring out portions and whether they have given themselves too much. Further down the line, when you are feeling more confident, you may feel more comfortable increasing the variety of your diet.

Once normal eating habits are restored, most people with bulimic anorexia will also stop purging, although some will need to make a special effort.

Improving your body image and self-esteem

We are all uniquely identified by our bodies and each one of us has plenty of thoughts and feelings about the one we inhabit – its size, shape, attractiveness, competence, health and so on. Research has shown that many people unfortunately find it hard to accept what they look like, creating a negative body image (the mental picture you have of your own body and how you think people see you). This results in feelings of depression, anxiety and social self-consciousness. A person with an eating disorder has a particularly difficult relationship with her body. Research shows that the disorder will almost certainly persist if greater body acceptance is not achieved.

You are likely to have acknowledged already that you have a poor body image and low self-esteem and would like these things to be different. Starting with body image, you are almost certainly intensely self-critical about your size and shape. You may even be so terrified, so fearful that you avoid touching your body or looking in the mirror. However, if you can improve your body image, you will automatically raise your self-esteem – your basic emotional sense of who you are.

Some people with anorexia avoid looking at themselves in the mirror, and therefore lose touch with how they appear. It is important to confront this as the more you avoid looking at yourself, the less you will actually know how you appear, and the larger you will imagine yourself to be.

Other people with anorexia stare at their bodies in a full-length mirror, disparaging what they see. They pinch whatever small amount of fat they think they can see and are convinced they are obese. These irrational thoughts must be addressed and the following exercises can help.

Things you can do to improve your body image

- Think of your positive qualities rather than just the things you don't like about yourself.
- Stand in front of a mirror and survey your reflection. You may immediately come up with a negative statement about your body, so compensate by making a positive one. There may not be much you like about yourself at this point, but do force yourself to find something. Every time you look in a mirror, do this for every negative statement you make. Now, most importantly, write down all your positive statements and, when you find yourself hating your body, read them through.
- When standing in front of a mirror, try not to focus on one part of your body as this exaggerates how it appears. Look at your body as a whole, as this is a more accurate representation of how you look.
- Do you look in the mirror one day and think you look OK, and the next day think you look awful? It's not your body that's changing; it's your perception of it that is. Try to notice your mood when you look in the mirror – it's odds on that you are feeling fairly content on the days you think

you look OK, and miserable on the days you think you look awful.

- Does your body image hold you back in any way? Do you avoid wearing skirts, looking in full-length mirrors, wearing swimsuits or using a communal changing room? People with eating disorders often worry about what others will think of them or how others will react if, for example, they wear a skirt. Try to challenge your body image by wearing a skirt and be aware of what actually happens. There is no reason for you to get a negative reaction. Write your answer in your notebook and keep referring to it. If you are a man, change the suggestions in this paragraph around so that it applies to you.

- Another way to challenge the distorted perception you have of yourself is to put two pieces of string on the floor, the same width apart as the size of a part of your body that you dislike, say a thigh. Then place your thigh down on to the pieces of string to see if you have estimated its width accurately. You probably made the string much further apart than the width of your thigh, but now you can see with your own eyes that you were mistaken. You could ask a trusted friend to help you with parts of your body that you can't see so easily.

- Once you embark on the recovery journey, do not torture yourself by hanging on to old clothes that no longer fit. Let them go and throw them out!

Dealing with anxiety

Most people with anorexia suffer from anxiety. It can arise as a result of being unhappy about your body and weight, your general appearance, being locked into an unhealthy cycle of eating or not eating, worrying about what other people think of you or maybe feeling isolated from family and friends. If you are suffering from anorexia, it is likely that every time you eat, you feel scared and anxious about whether you are allowed to eat this particular food, and how it will affect your weight. Every time you are weighed you are likely to feel scared and anxious about whether your weight has gone up and whether you look fat. Every time you see someone you know, you are likely to feel scared and anxious about what they are thinking about you, whether they are going to suggest that you eat something with them or whether they think you've put on weight.

Anxiety has the effect of stimulating the sympathetic nervous system – the mechanisms in the brain that respond automatically to certain occurrences – making you more tense and tired, and more anxious than previously. To help you relax, it's worth trying to follow a regular deep breathing and relaxation routine (see the section on 'Relaxation' later in this chapter).

When you find yourself in a difficult situation – with people you haven't seen for a long time, for example – it's helpful to challenge yourself and stay just where you are, however

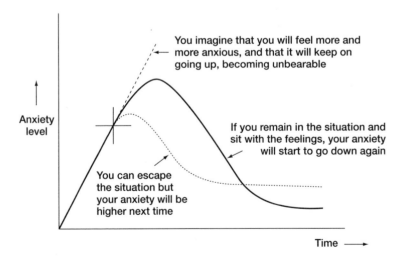

Understanding anxiety levels

uncomfortable you may feel. In remaining within the situation, you will learn that eventually it does become tolerable and that your anxiety levels will gradually decrease. It is hard to believe you can bear the anxiety and that it will decrease rather than continuing to increase. However, given time, this is what happens. If you avoid the situation, your anxiety will actually be worse the next time you are faced with a similar situation as you will be feeling even more strongly that the only way out is to 'escape'.

Understanding anxiety will help you challenge the things that cause you fear and anxiety. For example, if you worry about finishing everything on your plate, you will find yourself at the anxiety crossroads shown above. At this point you can choose the 'escape' road by leaving some food, gaining immediate relief from the discomfort you feel, or the 'sitting with your feelings' road, continuing to eat and bearing the discomfort. The latter will result in a reduction in anxiety over time. However, if you have taken the escape route, this will cause the next meal to be even harder, as your anxiety will be even greater and you will probably feel that you need to leave more food in order to feel better again. You can see how anxiety becomes a vicious cycle, in turn producing more anxiety.

Panic attacks

Acute hyperventilation or overbreathing – more commonly known as a panic attack – is fairly common in people with anorexia. A panic attack is an emotional response to anticipated stress. Often the perceived threat is obvious, but sometimes there is no apparent reason for the onset of panicky feelings. In the latter instance, the reason may be buried in earlier life events. Talking to a counsellor or therapist may unlock buried fears and help you to see them in a new, more manageable light.

As a panic attack builds, your anxiety intensifies. You start breathing faster in troubled apprehension. Light-headedness, palpitations, sweating, and the sensation that your chest is tightening are accompanied by feelings of inadequacy, fear, maybe of impending doom.

Daily deep breathing exercises – where breathing is slowed down and, on inhalation, the abdomen (not the rib-cage) is allowed to rise – are very useful training. An immediate remedy is the good old paper bag. As soon as your breathing becomes fast and shallow, place the paper bag over your nose and mouth and try to breathe more slowly. Breathing into the bag will ensure that most of the carbon dioxide you exhale is returned to your lungs. It will also calm down your breathing.

Relaxation

People with stress-related problems like insomnia, anxiety and depression can have an oversensitive stress response and higher levels of stress hormones in their bloodstream than others. This can affect your brain chemistry and be one factor in triggering and maintaining chronic stress, anxiety and depression. A useful strategy to learn is relaxation, as it helps to halt the arousal of the sympathetic nervous system.

What actually is relaxation?

Many people think relaxation is sitting with their feet up watching the television or reading a book, but this is not strictly so. It is impossible to obtain the same beneficial biochemical and physiological changes while watching some TV or reading a book as you do when practising relaxation. Indeed, research using electroencephalogram (EEG) monitors to record the brainwave patterns of people watching television and others using a relaxation technique show that practising relaxation causes the brain to produce alpha type brain waves that indicate true relaxation.

Deep breathing

In normal breathing, we take oxygen from the atmosphere down into our lungs. The diaphragm contracts and air is pulled into the chest cavity. When we breathe out, we expel carbon dioxide and other waste gases back into the atmosphere. However, when we are stressed or upset, we tend to use our rib muscles to expand the chest. We breathe more quickly, sucking in air shallowly. This is good in a crisis as it allows us to obtain the optimum amount of oxygen in the shortest possible time, providing our bodies with the extra power needed to handle the emergency. But some people get stuck in chest-breathing mode. Long-term shallow breathing is not only detrimental to our physical and emotional health; it can also lead to hyperventilation, panic attacks, chest pains, dizziness and gastro-intestinal problems.

If you are breathing quickly and shallowly, it is recommended that you follow this deep breathing exercise:

A deep breathing exercise

The following exercise should, ideally, be performed daily:

1 Make yourself comfortable in a warm room where you know you will be alone for at least half an hour.
2 Close your eyes and try to relax.
3 Gradually slow down your breathing, inhaling and exhaling as evenly as possible.
4 As you inhale, allow your abdomen to swell upward. (Your chest should barely move.)
5 As you exhale, let your abdomen flatten.

Give yourself a few minutes to get into a smooth, easy rhythm. As worries and distractions arise, don't hang on to them. Wait calmly for them to float out of your mind – then focus once more on your breathing.

Visualize a square. Move along the top of the square as you inhale, then down one side as you exhale, along the bottom as you inhale and then up the other side as you exhale. Repeat so that you are tracking the square in time with the rhythm of your deep breathing. Focusing in this way may help you to avoid thinking about other things, and assist you to relax.

When you feel ready to end the exercise, open your eyes. Allow yourself enough time to become alert before rolling on to one side and getting up.

With practice, you will begin breathing with your diaphragm quite naturally – and in times of stress, you should be able to correct your breathing without too much effort.

A relaxation exercise

When you feel that you have reached an easy breathing rhythm, you can go on to the following relaxation exercise:

As you continue to breathe slowly and evenly, imagine yourself surrounded, perhaps, by lush, peaceful countryside, beside a gently trickling stream – or maybe on a deserted tropical beach, beneath swaying palm fronds, listening to the sounds of the ocean, thousands of miles from your worries and cares. Let the warm sun, the gentle breeze, and the peacefulness of it all wash over you ...

The tranquillity you feel at this stage can be enhanced by frequently repeating the exercise – once or twice a day is best. Given sufficient time, you should be able to switch into a calm state of mind whenever you feel stressed. Improved breathing leads to better circulation and oxygenation which, in turn, helps the muscles and connective tissues. A relaxed mind can also greatly aid concentration and short-term memory.

Improving your relationships

It is important to consider how your personal relationships might be affected by your anorexia. Some of you may have been able to preserve your relationships intact, but many others will have distanced yourselves both physically and emotionally. On the other hand, relationship problems may have triggered your condition in the first place. Although it is advisable to explore this situation with a professional within treatment, there are some things that you can try in order to help yourself.

Assessing your relationships

If you wish to improve your relationships with family members who are not living with you but with whom you were once close, this may be a good time to renew contact. If visiting them is too daunting, try a phone call. The chat may lead to a meeting, at which you will have an opportunity to rebuild your relationship with that particular person.

Where past friends are concerned, it would be wise first of all to assess whether their presence in your life was worthwhile. Was it an equal relationship, or did you find yourself making more effort than your friend? For example, were you the one who did all the running? Were you there to comfort your friend more than he or she was there to comfort you? If so, you may wish to follow some of the assertiveness steps listed in the following section on 'Expressing yourself assertively' to try to improve this relationship. If there is no change, you might choose not to reinstate the friendship. However, if the friend was there for you as much as you were there for them, you will perhaps want to contact them again. If even a phone call seems too difficult, you could write a letter or send an email, which would give you the chance to explain your problems with anorexia, and let them know that you are now on the road to recovery.

Assess all your past friendships in this way, and then review your current relationships with family and friends. Many people with anorexia think that they have succeeded in hiding their struggles with food from the people close to them. However, this is often not the case and friends and family have noticed the changes in the personality and behaviour of the person with anorexia as food takes over her life. Weight loss is also difficult to conceal, but friends and relatives may not feel able to broach the subject themselves. Speaking openly of your struggles will have the effect of bringing others closer. Having a rich and balanced network of relationships can be an enormous support, and is one of the most important ways to restore your wellbeing and good psychological health.

When assessing your relationships, it is important to consider your own behaviour and the impact that it has on each relationship.

Passive and aggressive behaviour

Have you ever found yourself wanting to say something to someone but not doing so in order to avoid confrontation? Have you ever been asked to do something, wanted to say no but ended up saying yes? People with anorexia often display passive behaviour, trying to please others at the expense of what they want themselves. As a result they become invisible, as decisions are made for them and nobody really knows their likes, dislikes, needs and priorities.

You may have done something that you did not want to do and to which you could not say no, but sabotaged it so that it was not successful or made sarcastic comments to convey what you really felt. People often use roundabout ways of getting what they want, without talking openly about their needs. They behave in an indirectly aggressive manner, taking an inferior stance yet attempting to punish or undermine the other person to get what they want. They may use guilt, sarcasm or other indirect methods to get their message across.

Maybe you have felt very angry and allowed things to build up, feeling unable to say anything, until you had a violent outburst. When someone becomes aggressive (threatening, demanding), there is no room for effective communication. Aggressive behaviour is self-serving and involves you focusing only on your own feelings and needs, forcing other people to give you what you want without considering their rights. Although you end up with what you wanted, this method of communicating can be very damaging to your relationships in the long term.

Expressing yourself assertively

Being assertive is about conveying what you want in an honest, direct and open way, without using inappropriate emotional leverage. It is based on the principle that you are a person of worth and are entitled to have opinions and enjoy life, as are others around you. Some people think that being assertive is selfish. However, the opposite is true: assertiveness acknowledges the importance of your rights, needs and feelings as well as those of the other person.

Being assertive is not always easy, but with practice, the following points will help you to communicate in a clear, honest and direct way:

- Be clear as to what you want and how you are feeling about the situation.
- Choose an appropriate time and a place to have the conversation (i.e. not when you're feeling upset).
- Use appropriate body language: make sure that you are both at the same level (i.e. both sitting or both standing); maintain eye contact.
- Don't rush what you're saying or raise your voice.
- Say what you want clearly and concisely; keep calm and to the point.
- Explain how the situation is making you feel without attacking or blaming the other person.
- Use specific examples.
- Use 'I' and 'we' instead of 'you' when talking about feelings.
- Aim to work cooperatively with the other person to reach a win-win situation; explain the mutual benefits of adopting your suggestion.
- If the other person objects, keep repeating your point while listening to his or her opinion.

- If the other person becomes aggressive, try not to be side-tracked. Instead, stick to the point and state that you will deal with other issues later. If need be, repeat yourself.
- If the other person tries to create a diversion, calmly point this out and repeat your message.
- Don't use passive behaviour, such as pleading or whining.
- Listen to what the other person has to say.
- Ask if you are unsure of anything.
- Ask the other person for feedback – for what he or she thinks – to try to get a dialogue going, rather than a one-sided conversation.
- Thank the other person for listening to your concerns.

People with anorexia often struggle to believe that their feelings and opinions are as important as those of people around them. It can often seem more important to keep a relationship than to express dissatisfaction or confront the other person. However, this leads to unequal relationships, which can be a source of unhappiness and can serve to maintain anorectic thinking. Anorexia can arise when parents find it difficult to express their feelings towards a susceptible child. Ongoing communication difficulties can then perpetuate the problem, whether the child is still a child, or now an adult.

Encouraging someone close to change

In order to help your family to begin speaking openly, it can be a good idea to ask your doctor for a referral to a family therapy unit. It is also worth putting into practice the suggestions on assertiveness mentioned in the previous section. If, say, you feel that difficulties in communication between your family and yourself are the root cause of a lot of your troubles, it may only serve to alienate your family further. However, you could say for example, 'We don't often talk to each other about how we feel if we have problems and so on – but I would really like it if we could try to. I think that would help me to conquer my anorexia. What do you think?' They may be open to the idea, or you might find that they respond defensively. Remember, though, the communication patterns in your family will have developed over many years and so will not change immediately.

If you feel family members or close friends contribute by their behaviour to your anorexia, speak to them about it. It's not always possible or healthy to remove such people from your life, but you can try to encourage them to change. It's easy to see how others can misunderstand or take offence when we fail to communicate effectively, but changing the habits of a lifetime is difficult. It means analysing your thoughts before rearranging them into speech. You will be rewarded for your efforts, however, when people start to listen, when they start to support you in your efforts to conquer your anorexia. Most of all, if their behaviour has contributed to your problem, speaking carefully to them about it can make all the difference. If it doesn't, don't forget that your doctor can refer you and your family to a local family unit for therapy.

Problem solving

A person with anorexia may binge-eat or starve herself further in response to a problem. Often the problem is obvious, but at other times it may be difficult to ascertain what exactly is bothering you. You may know only that you feel anxious and unhappy and are therefore more susceptible to the impulse to binge or starve, or to feel unsightly. It is therefore essential that you try to identify the problem.

You can learn to deal with problems by following these steps:

• Think hard about what the problem actually is, and then write it down as clearly as possible on a page at the back of your notebook.

- Contemplate all the possible solutions to your problem, wild as some of them may seem. Write them all down.
- Look hard at all the solutions, thinking of what exactly is involved. Decide which of your solutions you could most realistically go ahead with, and whether it could be effective.
- Act on the solution you have chosen.
- After the event, look at what has happened and consider whether your solution was effective. If things didn't work out, reflect on what you might have done to produce a better outcome.

This problem-solving technique is widely used and with great success. In time, working out solutions will become second nature. You should even be able to break destructive cycles in close relationships, helping you to feel happier and more capable in your life.

Challenging negative thinking

We don't normally question our own thinking – we're often not even aware of the thoughts running around in our heads. However, when our thoughts are very negative we tend to believe they are accurate and true, and that can fuel problematic behaviour. For instance, a man who thinks he's no good with money will stop trying to be good with money; a girl who's convinced she'll fail her exams might not revise and so may then fail her exams. These negative thoughts are irrational untruths that determine our behaviour and even the paths our lives take.

The following automatic thoughts and beliefs are examples of the internal world of a person with anorexia:

- I hate my body. If I lost some weight, people would like me more.
- My life would be far better if I were slim.
- Being so fat makes me feel useless.
- I'll never look the way I want to look.

Luckily, such irrational thoughts and beliefs can be turned around. It is possible to learn a new, more positive approach to life. First, you need to acknowledge your irrational thoughts and beliefs for what they are, and for the behaviour they induce. Writing down your negative thoughts and feelings in your notebook, and really analysing them, can make the fact that they are irrational crystal clear. It makes you more aware.

Here is an example of possible irrational thoughts and feelings prior to a family party, an event that commonly provokes great anxiety in people with anorexia:

Situation	Irrational thoughts	Irrational feelings
Family Party	They'll all think I'm hideous because I'm so fat. No one will want to talk to me. I'll spoil the whole event.	Sad, alienated

The example illustrates just how irrational anorexia can make a person's thoughts. Yet without analysis, the potential repercussions can be staggering. By noticing your automatic negative thoughts and how they influence what you then do, you will see how sometimes you are making assumptions about what others will think or do, or you may be setting up these worst-case scenarios to actually happen. For example, isolating yourself at a party because of the way you feel about yourself and your weight may cause others to think that they have done something to upset you or that you are not enjoying the party. This may in turn cause an atmosphere or even an argument. Alternatively, you may end up talking yourself into staying at home, experiencing mixed self-pity, guilt and self-loathing.

Try to imagine what your own thoughts and feelings would be prior to a family party, and then look objectively at what you have written. Are your thoughts and feelings reasonable? Do you ever know for certain what other people are thinking? It is easy to make assumptions about what they are thinking based on what we are thinking about ourselves. When we challenge negative feelings in this way, the reality of the situation soon becomes apparent.

So, you have re-evaluated and subsequently vanquished one set of negative thoughts – only to find it swiftly replaced by another. You have decided to attend the party, but now you are worrying about eating in company.

Writing down your thoughts helps you to see them in a more detached light, as you can see from the next example. Here, columns listing alternative thoughts and possible solutions have been added.

Situation	Irrational thoughts	Irrational feelings	Alternative thoughts	Solution
Buffet at the family party	If I eat in front of my family they will think I'm greedy and shouldn't be eating because I'm so fat.	Ashamed	I'm making assumptions about what others are thinking – I can't mind read! Others are watching me around food because they are worried about me and want me to eat.	Stick to the meal plan and remember why I'm doing it. If I know I won't be able to eat at the party, make sure I eat before I go, or take something 'safe' to eat with me.

When you next come across a dilemma and start thinking irrationally, write down your thoughts, look at them with detachment and see them for what they really are. If they truly are irrational, try to think of a solution. Whether you are able to act on that solution is another matter – but the more you set your mind to thinking of solutions, the easier it will be to act on them.

Keep the notebook close at hand and try to get into the habit of writing down all your negative thoughts as they pass through your mind. See each one from different perspectives and decide honestly whether it is irrational. If it is, think of the irrational feelings such a thought might provoke, and of course the resulting behaviour. Recognizing negative thoughts for what they are is another great leap along that road to recovery.

Recovery maintenance

The nature of anorexia makes for a rocky road to recovery. Most of you will experience setbacks, whether you are helping yourselves or following trained guidance. However, it's more likely that you'll be able to get back on track if you've already developed a plan of action. The following strategies may alert you to potential pitfalls and help to turn things around if they start to slide backwards.

It's normal for a person confronting anorexia to maintain a drive to starve, perhaps interspersed with periods of binge-eating and purging. If you have consistently surrendered to this drive, tell yourself you have a choice over whether you give in to it or whether you continue with your recovery programme. When your preoccupation with food is intense, or if you are feeling excessively anxious about your weight and shape, try to distract yourself and keep yourself busy.

One of the most commonly used distraction techniques is washing hair. It's always 'available' and you aren't reliant on anyone else. When you feel you can no longer cope with the negative feelings, it will push you out of the kitchen, and it isn't possible to wash hair and eat at the same time! It gives you time to collect and re-motivate yourself. It's also likely you'll look and feel better, improving your esteem.

Get yourself out of the kitchen or away from places where food is available so that the means to binge are not there. You could arrange to see a supportive friend or relative who can help you through times where you are tempted to slip back into old patterns. Otherwise, you might consider one of the following:

- listen to a relaxation tape or go through the relaxation technique described on pages 101–3, using visualization;

- listen to music that either stirs you or relaxes you;
- phone a friend or relative who makes you feel calm;
- write down how you are feeling;
- read a book;
- play a musical instrument;
- draw or paint.

Being aware of your triggers

Hopefully by this point you will have some ideas about when you are most vulnerable to use food to regain a sense of control. There may be certain circumstances that arouse painful feelings that you want to alleviate by using food. By being aware of when you are most at risk, you can put in place some safety measures to help you stick to your meal plan or stop you using compensatory behaviours. When you are in the moment it is more difficult, so think ahead and have a contingency plan.

For example, if you are going out for a drink with friends, you may find it difficult to have your snack with them or its timing might be altered, so you could take a snack bar with you to have when you need to. Or if you feel that you are tempted to make yourself sick after a particular meal, you could enlist the help of a friend or family member to distract you or get you out of the house and out of the danger area.

Reverting to your old ways of thinking

If you find yourself constantly falling back into your old ways of negative thinking, take a look again at your diary and re-read your entries for 'Challenging negative thinking' and 'Problem solving'. It's not easy to change entrenched thought patterns, but it can be done. Remember that with a little effort now, you will learn to see yourself in a more positive light, and that will help you to achieve a better body image.

On days when everything feels overwhelming, it might be useful to have a letter that you have written to yourself when you were feeling more positive, containing some reminders of your strengths, abilities, successes and strategies for carrying on the fight. Remind yourself of what you've already achieved and how things could be if you keep going.

Self-help groups

There are now anorexia self-help groups in many areas. (See page 117 of the 'Useful addresses' section at the back of the book.) The advantages of attending such a group are as follows:

- You don't feel like a patient with a 'sickness', unlike when you attend a hospital.
- Everyone at the group is in the same situation.
- There may be group members who are available at all times via a telephone helpline, acting as crisis management for their fellow sufferers.
- Members act as a general support network for each other. Those who can actually offer help give their self-esteem a great boost.
- Self-help groups also offer the opportunity to make new friends who you can see socially, out of the group.

Although self-help groups can offer invaluable encouragement to a person with anorexia, it's important that you don't depend on them entirely for guidance and support. Self-help groups can, however, be a beneficial adjunct to the advice in this book. You can also attend a self-help group while receiving treatment from a professional.

And lastly ...

If after reading this book you feel you cannot follow its recommendations, don't be dispirited. Always remember it is never too late to recover. You must get help, however. Talk to your family. In addition, talk to your GP. He or she will know the best sources of professional help in your area. Good luck!

Appendix: Weight charts

Metres	1.42	1.45	1.47	1.50	1.52	1.55	1.58	1.60	1.63	1.65	1.68	1.70	1.73	1.75	1.78
Feet/inches	4'8"	4'9"	4'10"	4'11"	5'0"	5'1"	5'2"	5'3"	5'4"	5'5"	5'6"	5'7"	5'8"	5'9"	5'10"
Age															
15	38.1	39.9	41.7	43.5	45.4	47.2	49.0	50.8	52.2	54.0	55.8	57.6	59.4	61.2	63.0
16	40.8	42.2	44.0	45.4	47.2	48.5	50.3	51.7	53.5	54.9	56.7	58.1	59.9	61.2	63.0
17	42.6	44.0	45.8	47.2	48.5	49.9	51.3	53.1	54.4	55.8	57.2	58.5	60.3	61.7	63.0
18	43.5	44.9	46.3	47.6	49.4	50.8	52.2	53.5	54.9	56.7	58.1	59.4	60.8	62.1	64.0
19	44.0	45.4	46.7	48.1	49.9	51.3	52.6	54.0	55.3	57.2	58.5	59.9	61.2	62.6	64.4
20	44.5	45.8	47.2	48.5	49.9	51.7	53.1	54.4	55.8	57.2	59.0	60.3	61.7	63.0	64.4
21	44.5	45.8	47.2	49.0	50.3	51.7	53.1	54.4	56.2	57.6	59.0	60.3	61.7	63.5	64.9
22	44.5	46.3	47.6	49.0	50.3	51.7	53.5	54.9	56.2	57.6	59.0	60.8	62.1	63.5	64.9
23	44.5	46.3	47.6	49.0	50.3	51.7	53.5	54.9	56.2	57.6	59.0	60.8	62.1	63.5	64.9
24	44.9	46.3	48.1	49.4	50.8	52.2	53.5	54.9	56.2	57.6	59.0	60.3	61.7	63.5	64.9
27	45.4	46.7	48.1	49.4	50.8	52.6	54.0	55.3	56.7	58.1	59.4	60.8	62.1	63.5	65.3
32	46.7	48.1	49.4	50.8	52.2	53.5	54.9	56.2	57.6	59.0	60.3	61.7	63.0	64.4	65.8
37	48.1	49.4	50.8	52.2	53.5	54.9	56.2	57.6	59.0	60.3	61.7	63.0	64.4	65.8	67.1
42	50.3	51.7	53.1	54.4	55.8	57.2	58.5	59.9	60.8	62.1	63.5	64.9	66.2	67.6	68.9
47	52.2	53.5	54.4	55.8	57.2	58.5	59.9	61.2	62.6	64.0	65.3	66.2	67.6	68.9	70.3
52	53.1	54.4	55.8	57.2	58.1	59.4	60.8	62.1	63.5	64.4	65.8	67.1	68.5	69.9	70.8
57	53.1	54.4	55.8	57.2	58.5	59.4	60.8	62.1	63.5	64.9	65.8	67.1	68.5	69.9	71.2
62	52.6	54.0	55.3	56.2	57.6	59.0	60.3	61.7	62.6	64.0	65.3	66.7	68.0	68.9	70.3
67	51.3	52.6	54.0	55.3	56.2	57.6	59.0	60.3	61.7	62.6	64.0	65.3	66.7	68.0	68.9

Height

Graduated mean weights (kgs) at each age and height: females

		Height													
Metres	1.52	1.55	1.58	1.60	1.63	1.65	1.68	1.70	1.73	1.75	1.78	1.80	1.83	1.85	1.88
Feet/inches	5' 0"	5' 1"	5' 2"	5' 3"	5' 4"	5' 5"	5' 6"	5' 7"	5' 8"	5' 9"	5' 10"	5' 11"	6' 0"	6' 1"	6' 2"
Age															
15	43.5	45.8	47.6	49.4	51.3	53.1	55.3	57.2	59.0	60.8	62.6	64.9	66.7	68.5	70.3
16	44.9	47.2	49.0	50.8	52.6	54.4	56.2	58.1	59.9	61.7	63.5	66.2	67.6	69.4	71.2
17	46.7	48.5	50.3	52.2	54.4	55.8	57.6	59.4	61.2	63.0	64.9	66.7	68.5	70.3	72.1
18	48.1	49.9	51.3	53.1	54.9	56.7	58.5	60.3	62.1	64.0	65.8	67.1	68.9	70.8	72.6
19	49.4	50.8	52.6	54.4	56.2	58.1	59.9	61.2	63.0	64.9	66.7	68.0	69.9	71.7	73.5
20	50.3	52.2	54.0	55.3	57.2	59.0	60.8	62.1	64.0	65.8	67.1	68.9	70.8	72.1	73.9
21	51.7	53.1	54.9	56.2	58.1	59.9	61.2	63.0	64.4	66.2	68.0	69.4	71.2	72.6	74.4
22	52.2	54.0	55.3	57.2	59.0	60.3	62.1	63.5	65.3	67.1	68.5	70.3	71.7	73.5	75.3
23	52.6	54.4	56.2	57.6	59.4	60.8	62.6	64.4	65.8	67.6	68.9	70.8	72.6	73.9	75.8
24	53.1	54.9	56.2	58.1	59.9	61.2	63.0	64.4	66.2	68.0	69.4	71.2	72.6	74.4	76.2
27	53.5	54.9	56.7	58.5	59.9	61.7	63.5	65.3	66.7	68.5	70.3	71.7	73.5	75.3	76.7
32	54.4	55.8	57.6	59.4	60.8	62.6	64.4	66.2	67.6	69.4	71.2	72.6	74.4	76.2	78.0
37	54.9	56.2	58.1	59.9	61.7	63.0	64.9	66.7	68.0	69.9	71.7	73.5	74.8	76.7	78.5
42	54.9	56.7	58.1	59.9	61.7	63.0	64.9	66.7	68.0	69.9	71.7	73.5	74.8	76.7	78.5
47	55.3	56.7	58.5	60.3	61.7	63.5	65.3	67.1	68.5	70.3	72.1	73.5	75.3	77.1	78.9
52	55.3	57.2	59.0	60.8	62.1	64.0	65.8	67.1	68.9	70.8	72.1	73.9	75.8	77.1	78.9
57	55.8	57.6	59.4	60.8	62.6	64.4	66.2	67.6	69.4	71.2	72.6	74.4	76.2	77.6	79.4
62	56.2	58.1	59.9	61.2	63.0	64.9	66.2	68.0	69.9	71.7	73.0	74.8	76.7	78.0	79.8
67	56.7	58.5	60.3	61.7	63.5	65.3	66.7	68.5	70.3	71.7	73.5	75.3	77.1	78.5	80.3

Graduated mean weights (kgs) at each age and height: males

Useful addresses

The essential first point of contact for people with anorexia is **beat** (formerly the Eating Disorders Association), a UK-based charitable organization that offers information, help and assistance to clients, carers and professionals.

UK and Ireland

Anorexia & Bulimia Care (ABC)
PO Box 173
Letchworth
Herts SG6 1XQ
Tel.: 01462 423351
Website: www.anorexiabulimiacare.co.uk

A Christian organization for people with eating disorders, and their carers.

beat (formerly the Eating Disorders Association)
First Floor, Wensum House
103 Prince of Wales Road
Norwich NR1 1DW
Helplines: 0845 634 1414; 0845 634 7650 (for young people)
Website: www.b-eat.co.uk
Email: help@b-eat.co.uk

A charitable organization that offers information, help and assistance to clients, carers and professionals.

Bodywhys – The Eating Disorders Association Of Ireland
PO Box 105
Blackrock
Co. Dublin
Helpline: 1890 200 444
Website: www.bodywhys.ie

An Irish national charity that provides information and support to people with eating disorders, and their families.

Mental Health Foundation (London Office)
Ninth Floor, Sea Containers House
20 Upper Ground
London SE1 9QB
Website: www.mentalhealth.org.uk

A UK charity providing information on mental-health issues, including eating disorders. There is a Scottish office at 30 George Square, Glasgow G2 1EG.

St George's National Eating Disorders Service
S.W. London and St George's NHS Trust
Springfield University Hospital
Harewood House
61 Glenburnie Road
London SW17 7DJ
Tel.: 020 8725 5528/9; 020 7535 7706
Website: www.swlstg-tr.nhs.uk/specialities/eating_disorders.asp

The largest service in the UK providing assessment, care and treatment for adults, adolescents and children with eating disorders who are referred through Community NHS Mental Health Teams nationwide.

Samaritans
Chris
PO Box 90 90
Stirling FK8 2SA
Tel.: 08457 90 90 90 (free)
Website: www.samaritans.org.uk
Email: jo@samaritans.org

USA

National Eating Disorders Association
603 Stewart Street, Suite 803
Seattle
WA 98101
Toll-free information and referral helpline: (800) 931-2237
Website: www.edap.org
Email: info@NationalEatingDisorders.org

Websites

BBC Website
www.bbc.co.uk/health

Contains information in the mental-health section on eating disorders.

Counselling Ltd
www.counselling.ltd.uk

A charity which puts people in touch with counsellors in their area, some offering free or low-cost services.

Mental Health Care

www.mentalhealthcare.org.uk

A resource website run by the Institute of Psychiatry.

Mirror-Mirror

www.mirror-mirror.org

An American website that provides, on a self-help basis, information on eating disorders, getting help, recovery, etc., as well as links to other websites.

Index

affective disorder 5
age 2
alcohol 24–5
anorexia nervosa: causes of 35–44;
definition and symptoms 1–5;
historical view 9–10; physical
effects of 46–7; professional care
for 4; reversible health 33–4; signs
of 27–8, 45–8; statistics of 2, 5–7;
triggers 113; *see also* body image;
recovery; treatment; weight
anxiety 98–101
appetite loss, non-anorexic 4–5, 18–19
Attention Deficit Hyperactivity
Disorder (ADHD) 51–2

binge-eating 1–2, 19, 55, 89, 112
body image: anxiety about 12,
38, 40–1, 85; children and 38;
improving 96–8; men 80–1;
mothers and 56–60; psychotherapy
for 77; self-esteem 96; signs of
anorexia 45–6; social pressure
38–40, 41–2; work and 5–6
bone demineralization 3, 23, 29–30
Bruch, Dr Hilde 9
bulimia nervosa 5, 19, 67; compared
to anorexia 2–3; defined 1–2; *see
also* binge-eating
bullying 43

children 30, 42–3; Food Avoidance
Emotional Disorder 5; individual
identity of 35–7; in-patient
treatment 79–80; *see also* families
clothing 23–4, 46, 98
cognitive-behavioural therapy 72–3
community mental health teams
(CMHT) 64–5

constipation 33
creative activities 76–7
Crisp, Arthur 9

dance 6
depression 16, 46, 84, 94;
antidepressants 73–4
diabetes 51, 84
digestive system 20–1, 32–3
diuretics 3, 21
dizziness 47
doctors 8, 64, 83–4
drugs: abusing 24–5; antidepressants
73–4; diet pills 18–19; emetics 21;
overdosing 26

eating *see* food and eating
Eating Disorder Not Otherwise
Specified (EDNOS) 1–2
emotions 16, 18–19, 62–3, 94; coping
with motherhood 52–60; mood
swings 12; self-assessment 85; *see
also* depression
environmental factors 7, 42–3
exercise: excessive 3, 21–2, 46;
healthy amounts 60, 77–8;
monitoring 88; during pregnancy
55; side-effects from pills 18–19

facial expressions 16
families: adolescents and identity
35–7; anorexia within 6–7;
communication 106–7; mothers
and 51–2, 56–80; parental role 7;
self-esteem and 37; therapy 71–2
fashion industry 6
food and eating 4, 42–3, 75; eating
habits 88; hidden 46; maintaining
recovery 112–14; meal plans 91–4;

monitoring 88–90; normal eating 93; preoccupation with 12, 13–14; restriction 17–18; types and amounts 94–6
Food Avoidance Emotional Disorder 5

gender 5–6; cultural views of women 39–40; male anorexia 6, 8–9, 80–1
genetic factors 7, 43–4
Gull, Sir William 9

hair, fine body/lanugo 28, 47
heart function 32
hormones 29, 50

identity, adolescent 35–7
immune system 31

kidney function 33

laxatives 3, 20–1, 46, 88
libido see sex

memory 16
menstruation: irregular or stopped 2, 3, 28–9, 47, 49; return of 87–8; self-harm and 25
minerals 55; in bones 3, 23, 29–30
multi-impulsive behaviour 24
muscle wastage 31
music industry 6

National Institute of Clinical Excellence 69

oedema 27, 47, 90–1
osteopenia 29–30

panic attacks 100–1
perfectionism 14–15, 46, 83
Pervasive Refusal Syndrome 5
pregnancy and motherhood 49–56, 84; accidental 50; relationship with your child 57–60
problem solving 108–9
psychological treatment: anger management 77; body awareness 77; cognitive-behavioural therapy 72–3; counselling 54; creative activities 76–7; dialectical behaviour therapy 71; family therapy 71–2; group sessions 74–5, 77; harm reduction 78–9; healthy exercise 77–8; in-patient 67; living skills and cookery 75; motivational work 70–1; psychodynamic therapy 71

recovery 61–4, 84–6; eating and 90–6, 112–14; helping yourself 82–3; professional help 83–4; target weight 68–70
relaxation 101–3, 112–13
reproductive system 3, 28–9, 34, 49–52, 54; see also menstruation; pregnancy and motherhood
ritualistic behaviour 12, 14
Russell, Gerald 9
Russell's sign 19–20, 47

salivary glands 3, 47
self-esteem 12, 24, 37, 85, 96–8; asserting yourself 106–7; multi-impulsive behaviour 24; sexual activity and 26
self-harm 25, 84
self-help 82, 88–96
self-help groups 114
sex 26, 42; abuse 43; loss of drive 2, 28
skin 3, 19–20, 27, 46–7
sleep disturbance 3, 47
social relations 84; asserting yourself 106–7; assessing health of 104–5; dread of occasions 13–14; effect of anorexia on 103–4; help from 113; helping others 107–8; passive/aggressive behaviour 105–6; withdrawal 15, 46
sports 6, 8
swelling see oedema

teeth 3, 47
temperature sensitivity 23, 28
thinking and attitudes: asserting yourself 108–9; challenging negative thoughts 109–12, 113;

disturbed by low weight 16;
oversimplified 12; problem
solving 108–9; stereotyped 15;
typical anorexia 11–16
treatment 66; children 79–80;
day-patient 66–7; decision to
act 61–2; emotions of 62–3;
in-patient 67–8, 78–80; for men
80–1; naso-gastric feeding 68, 79;
out-patient 64–7; professional
help 83–4; psychological
interventions 70–4; supporting
teams 63, 64–5
twins 37

vomiting 3, 19–20, 21, 46, 47;
digestive system and 33; mineral
loss 32; monitoring 88

weight 2–5, 13; body mass index (BMI)
28, 48, 67, 87–8; charts 115–16;
food restriction 17–18; gaining
87–8, 90–1; keeping track of 47;
laxatives and 21; levels of 27–8;
severe malnutrition 27–34, 84;
signs of anorexia 45; social
contexts 38; targets 68–70, 87–8
Wilgefortis, St 9, 10
work 6